Breaking The Nation

Breaking The Nation
A guide to Thatcher's Britain

Written and researched by
Jane Ashley, Liz Atkins, Dick Barry, Geoff Bish,
Bert Clough, Julian Eccles, Mike Gapes, Sue Goss,
Jane Henderson, Tim Lamport, Tony Manwaring,
Jim Murphy, Jenny Pitkin, Gordon Prentice,
Nick Sigler

Edited by Tony Manwaring and Nick Sigler

Pluto  Press
and
New Socialist

First published in 1985 by Pluto Press Limited,
The Works, 105a Torriano Avenue, London NW5 2RX
and Pluto Press Australia Limited, PO Box 199, Leichhardt,
New South Wales 2040, Australia

Cover designed by James Beveridge

Phototypeset by AKM Associates (UK) Ltd,
Ajmal House, Hayes Road, Southall, London
Printed in Great Britain by Cox & Wyman Limited, Reading

ISBN 0 7453 0020 0

Jane Ashley, Liz Atkins, Dick Barry, Geoff Bish, Bert Clough, Julian Eccles,
Mike Gapes, Sue Goss, Jane Henderson, Tim Lamport, Tony Manwaring,
Jim Murphy, Jenny Pitkin, Gordon Prentice and Nick Sigler are researchers
for the Labour Party.

Contents

Acknowledgements

We would like to thank all those at *New Socialist* and Pluto Press – especially Neil Middleton and Charlotte Greig – who have made the publication of this book possible.

Special thanks go also to all members of the Labour Party's staff who did additional research and typed the manuscript: Mandy Bebber, Michelle Beard, Kim Blackman, Lesley Borlase, Pat Francis, Kim Garrett, Beverly Knowles, Ruby Ranaweera, Arlene Ryan and Tom Watson.

The Tory record is only half the story. If you want to know more about the other half – the socialist alternative – then contact:

> The Labour Party
> 150, Walworth Road
> London SE17 1JT
> Tel: 01 703 0833

Introduction

■ *It breaks my heart to see what is happening in our country today.*

> Harold Macmillan, House of Lords, November 1984

■ *Mrs Thatcher's government is stepping out to become the most inept since the war.*

> *The Economist*, 7 July 1984

Britain is a divided, demoralized, broken nation. Instead of heading for the twenty-first century, we are being plunged back into the dark days of the nineteenth century. Back to the days of the Victorian values so beloved of Margaret Thatcher. Six years of Tory government have left Britain a more uncaring, unproductive, unjust, unfair, undemocratic nation.

Ours has become a nation in which the jobless are pitted against the employed; where the poor get poorer, while the rich get richer; where the wealthier South prospers at the expense of the impoverished North; where the sick suffer to benefit the healthy.

In their 1979 general election manifesto, the Tories said that they were setting out to 'rebuild our economy and reunite a divided and disillusioned people'. They have achieved precisely the opposite. The economy has been shattered. The people are more divided, more disillusioned, than ever.

Each day of Tory government has meant:

- 1,000 people joining the dole queues;
- 1,500 people being added to the numbers on supplementary benefit;
- 30 companies going into liquidation;
- £30 million being added to taxes;
- £25 million of capital investment going overseas;
- prices rising, on average, by a penny in the pound every month.

1

But the division and destruction wrought by the Tories cannot be measured only in cold statistics, as damning as these are. Nor is the trail of devastation restricted to the nation's economic and social well-being. For the Tories have undermined our democracy, stripped us of our rights and jeopardized our security.

As Britain approaches the twenty-first century, we are surrounded by contradictions. We labour under the illusion that we live in a modern state. A country in which the bonanza of North Sea Oil would provide the means to build a flourishing modern economy, able to provide the resources to care for the less fortunate; to educate the young and the old; to build houses for the homeless; to provide proper care for the sick.

Instead, we see record levels of unemployment. We see £17 billion a year being squandered on keeping people out of work. We see the nation's assets being sold off to give handouts to the Tories' already rich friends, to provide short-term gains from long-term losses.

We see more than £3 billion of public money being thrown away in an attempt to defeat the miners, cruelly branded as 'the enemy within', whose only 'crime' is that they will not acquiesce in the destruction of their jobs and their communities.

We see a country that was once the workshop of the world turned into a penny-farthing corner shop, unable even to manufacture its most basic needs.

We see an economy, determined on some mystical, monetarist goal, which records the highest ever level of real interest rates and the lowest ever level of sterling.

We see £3 billion spent on the folly of 'Fortress Falklands' yet the welfare state, once the envy of the world, is starved of resources, undermined in its purpose. Hundreds, perhaps thousands, of the elderly die because they can't afford to heat their homes. The sick are denied hospital treatment because the government has forced cuts in services to meet some fictitious 'efficiency' criterion. University departments are closed, schools cannot afford the most basic equipment, nurseries are shut down for lack of funds.

Millions of people are homeless, or living in sub-standard accommodation, while nearly half a million building workers are forced on to the dole.

We are led to believe that the government is committed to democracy, to the rule of law, to the defence of the nation. But the reality is different. Local authorities are stripped of their democratically conferred power, elections are abandoned. Crime is on the up and the police are increasingly used against the people, not to protect them.

Basic rights won through years of struggle are now taken away. The position of women in society is worsened, not improved. Discrimination against ethnic minorities increases rather than diminishes.

Billions of pounds are squandered on nuclear weapons – which can never hope to defend us but only attract aggressors – while our conventional defence forces are depleted to pay the bills of nuclear folly.

What sort of government is it that:

● Forty years after the Education Act 1944 has created the conditions in which schools have to organize bingo sessions among their pupils in order to raise the money to pay for textbooks?
● Thirty five years after the establishment of the National Health Service has created the conditions in which a man is denied life-saving treatment because the 'quality of his life is not good enough'?
● Seventy years after the Trade Union Act 1913 has trade unions fined hundreds of thousands of pounds because their members exercise their right to strike?
● Sixty-five years after the abolition of child labour creates the conditions in which private contractors use schoolchildren to clean our hospitals?

It is a government made up of people who, on reading the social history of the nineteenth century, resolve not to make matters better, not to banish those dark ages for ever, but rather to recreate them.

3

Economic vandalism

● For the first time ever Britain now imports more manufactured goods than it manages to sell overseas – which has resulted in a worsening in Britain's balance of trade in manufactures of over £9,000 million between 1978 and 1984.

● Under the Tories investment in manufacturing has slumped by a quarter; manufacturing output has fallen by 9 per cent and industrial output is down by 6 per cent.

● Britain's worsening balance of payments crisis is being hidden by the inflow of revenues from North Sea Oil – which, at £380 per second, now account for 9 per cent of all government revenues, but which will not last for ever.

● Because of the appalling lack of training programmes, and despite the record levels of unemployment, many companies are having to import workers to provide the skills they need to carry on their businesses.

● Since the Tories came to power, the pound has fallen in value by 18 per cent compared with the 'basket' of major currencies and by 46 per cent against the dollar.

● In the biggest ever programme of asset-stripping, the government is selling off £10,000 million-worth of Britain's publicly owned industries to its friends in the City – with discounts which, so far, have amounted to £2,500 million, while the cost of selling British Telecom alone was in the region of £300 million in fees to banks, stockbrokers and advertisers.

Social services: destruction guaranteed

● The National Health Service needs an increase in resources of 1.5 per cent each year just to maintain present standards. But the Tories have undermined the ability of the NHS to provide good-quality care for all by failing to provide the resources needed to meet these increasing demands. The basic rationale of the NHS has been undermined by Tory policy of forcing health authorities to contract out services and encouraging private medicine. The government is moving towards two-tier health-care: a prosperous, well-provided private sector for the wealthy and healthy; an underfunded, demoralized public service for the rest.

● In 1983, for the first time ever, the government ordered staff cuts in the NHS. As a result, health authorities cut over 11,000 jobs in 1983–4, including over 3,000 nursing jobs. This is happening at a time when NHS staff are working under ever-increasing pressure, and when the rate of unemployment among nurses and midwives has doubled and among doctors has trebled.

● Each year 3,000 kidney patients die for lack of treatment. Yet just £50 million – one-sixth of the cost of selling off British Telecom – would pay for the necessary life-saving equipment.

● In England and Wales 1.25 million dwellings are unfit for human habitation; a further 2.5 million homes are seriously affected by damp. Yet less than 40,000 new council houses were started in 1984.

● The Tories have reversed a 60-year trend towards a more equal distribution of wealth: 1 per cent of the population own 20 per cent of the nation's wealth.

● Under the Tories, the proportion of male manual workers classified as low-paid has doubled from 10 per cent to 20 per cent. Among women, it's risen from 65 per cent to 80 per cent.

● After just two years of Tory government, an extra 4 million people had fallen below the poverty line – making 15 million in all.

● The Tories have cheated pensioners by breaking the link between pensions and earnings, by delaying the introduction of pensions upratings, and by altering the method by which pension increases are calculated.

● One in four of Britain's children are living in, or on the margins of, poverty.

● Nearly 0.5 million school-leavers have not had a job since leaving school.

Local democracy under threat

● Rate-capping has removed control of local government from the town halls to Whitehall.

• Democratically elected local authorities – the GLC and the metropolitan counties – are being swept away, against the clear wishes of the majority of the 18 million people affected.

•The abolition of the GLC and the metropolitan counties will mean that their functions will be taken over by a concoction of largely unelected and unrepresentative boards and quangos. While the government claims these anti-democratic measures will save £100 million, they are actually likely to *cost* about £70 million. And up to 9,000 jobs will be lost.

•Between 1979 and 1985 the real value of Exchequer grants to local authorities has been cut by over 12 per cent – a loss to the authorities of nearly £8.5 billion.

•In 1979 central government provided 61 per cent of local authority expenditure. By 1985 that figure will have dropped to 49 per cent, forcing local authorities to cut services and/or impose punitive rate increases. Household rates increased by 130 per cent in the five years to 1983–4.

Your rights in their hands

•The Tories' Employment and Trade Union Acts have stripped unions of the legal immunities they won in the nineteenth century; impeded the right to strike; restricted the right to picket; ended the right to fair wages; weakened the law on unfair dismissals; dictated how senior union officials should be elected; forced unions to ballot before each and every call for industrial action; and are a blatant attempt to prevent unions from involving themselves in any form of political activity whatsoever.

•The state is interfering increasingly in legitimate dissent. The mail of CND has regularly been tampered with. Groups that criticize the 'established order' are marked out for surveillance by the Special Branch, according to former Chief Constable, John Alderson.

•At GCHQ 7,000 women and men have been stripped of their right to belong to a trade union. Armed forces personnel are being prevented from taking part in the affairs of any political organization – even in their own time. Ministry of Defence civil servants are being vetted for sympathies with any organizations opposing government policies.

● A junior civil servant, Sarah Tisdall, was prosecuted by means of the totally discredited Section 2 of the Official Secrets Act. Her crime: to leak a memorandum to the Defence Secretary, which in no way threatened national security, but which merely caused the government acute embarrassment.

● The new Police and Criminal Evidence Act gives the police new and dramatically increased powers. Such as greater powers to stop and search, and to detain a suspect in police custody for four days. The Act also authorizes intimate body and strip searches. These powers were used even before the Act became law to restrict the movement of miners in the National Union of Mineworkers' dispute with the National Coal Board. Miners had their cars turned back over 100 miles from picketing points.

● The average waiting time for citizenship applications is about 12–15 months. But Zola Budd, the white South African athlete, was granted British citizenship in just ten days. Yet the grounds for her case – a desire to run in the Olympics – were far less important than the reasons for the majority of normal applications.

The following pages catalogue the record of this latter-day Dickensian administration. They spell out in horrific detail the extent to which a modern society has been torn to tatters by a government increasingly dictatorial in style, increasingly regressive and repressive in operation.

But it is not just the nation which is being broken and destroyed. The government becomes daily more at odds with every section of the community. Thatcher's cabinet is fast becoming divorced even from its own slavish supporters.

Tory Party backbenchers are continuously in revolt, egged on by a bevy of ex-ministers, many sacked by Thatcher herself. The country's bishops, never usually known for their collective censure of Toryism, are up in arms as they see the destruction being wrought throughout the land. Even the bedrock sections of Tory support are being spurned, their views reviled. Farmers, land-owners, peers, even City financiers have risen up in condemnation of this appalling government.

Even as its support disappears, this government brooks no opposition. Its dogmatism blinds it to all calls for reason. It marches on regardless. But the tragedy it has created will return to undo it.

1. The attack on local government

The attack on local democracy

■ *The Labour Party is the party of division. In its present form it represents a threat to the democratic values and institutions on which our parliamentary system is based. The GLC is typical of this new, modern, divisive version of socialism. It must be defeated. So we shall abolish the GLC.*

Norman Tebbit MP, 15 March 1984

Since taking office in 1979 the Tories have displayed a breathtaking contempt for local democracy – and for the British Constitution. The groundwork was laid by the first Thatcher administration which devised an impenetrable and punitive system of local government finance aimed at choking back local spending. But with the general election of June 1983 behind her, the attack has intensified.

The right to vote

The Tory manifesto made a fleeting reference to the abolition of the GLC and the six metropolitan counties. But the country was given no indication that the Tories planned to cancel the elections due in May 1985. The legislative vehicle for this major constitutional change was to be the Local Government (Interim Provisions) Bill, widely known as the 'Paving Bill' – portrayed by the government as a necessary but run-of-the-mill measure. The reality was different. According to a House of Commons Library paper (84/5): 'These arrangements are unique in modern local government organization in that full elections are to be cancelled to local authorities which are to continue for a period beyond the date of these elections.' The Paving Bill was to transfer responsibility for running the seven threatened authorities for the last

11 months of their existence to transitional councils whose members would be drawn from – and reflect the political balance of – the metropolitan district and London borough councils. Under this formula, political control of the GLC would pass to the Tories and, until the metropolitan district elections in May 1984, there were some doubts as to whether Merseyside and the West Midlands would retain Labour majorities.

Even many Tories found this unpalatable. On 9 May 1984 Geoffrey Rippon, ex-Secretary of State for the Environment, declared:

> It is abject, squalid and shameful that a Conservative government should come forward with a proposal that, whether accidental or otherwise, substitutes for a directly elected socialist authority . . . an independently nominated quasi-quango of another political party. There is no way in which that can be justified.

Edward Heath had voiced his concern on 11 April 1984:

> Worst of all . . . is the imposition by parliamentary diktat of a change of responsible party in London government. There cannot be any justification for that. It immediately lays the Conservative Party open to the charge of the greatest gerrymandering in the last 150 years of British history.

As early as 8 December 1983, cabinet ministers had been briefed to counter the charge of gerrymandering by claiming in their public statements that councillors 'had no legitimate role beyond May 1985 when their electoral mandate expires', and that the transitional councils were an unavoidable consequence of the abolition commitment. (Briefing for Cabinet Ministers on Local Government Policies: Memo from Patrick Jenkin MP to the Prime Minister, 8 December 1983.)

In truth, the cancellation of the elections was *deliberately engineered*. On 26 March 1984 the *Guardian* published extracts from the minutes of the cabinet committee on abolition of the GLC and metropolitan counties. On 20 September 1983, the Environment Secretary wrote to the Prime Minister:

> Elections to the GLC and MCCs are due in May 1985. The [ministerial] group are agreed that *they cannot be allowed to go ahead*: other objections apart, abolition would be a major issue in the elections, so that there would be a major public debate going on after the House of Commons had voted for a second reading of the Abolition Bill.

Two options were outlined: (1) defer the elections; and (2) substitute borough and district councillors for the retiring GLC and metropolitan councillors. The minute goes on:

> A small majority of the group considered that both our own supporters and the wider public would find it incomprehensible that we should, in effect, extend the terms of office of the GLC and the Mets. Moreover, to do so would provide those bodies with *scope for obstruction* at a time when this would be most damaging to our policies. They therefore favoured substitition . . . In political terms this is probably one of the most sensitive decisions we have to take. My own recommendation is in favour of substitution. I propose we should announce this in the White Paper.

The **Paving Bill** was given its second reading in the Commons on 11 April 1984, with 19 Tories voting against – including Edward Heath and a clutch of former cabinet ministers – and survived a further challenge in the Lords at second reading. Throughout this period, government ministers emphasized that there was no alternative to cancelling the elections.

During the debate, Environment Minister William Waldegrave explained why an extension of the term was not possible: 'They [the councillors] would not have been elected and they would have no mandate. They would be appointed [by the Secretary of State] for an extra year for which they had not been elected . . . To do that would be wrong. I have to say that it would be extremely foolish.'

The whole carefully planned exercise came unstuck in the Lords on 28 June 1984 when Labour and crossbench peers joined Tory rebels to reject the cancellation of the elections. The government backed down and extended the term of the GLC and metropolitan councillors to April 1986 – the abolition date. This was the cue for Conservative Central Office to ridicule the notion of having *any* elections in the areas threatened with abolition.

In order to test public opinion in London on the question of abolition, four Labour GLC councillors resigned their seats, so forcing by-elections. The government tried to write off these elections as a stunt – and London Tories were ordered not to contest the seats. But it was left to Tory GLC councillor George Tremlett to say publicly what many voters were thinking in private. The *Standard* (19 September 1984) published his comments:

> Twice in recent days the *Standard* has published editorials urging the GLC Conservative Group to sack me . . . My offence is that I have urged people to vote Labour in tomorrow's four by-elections. I am totally unrepentant. *It is the Labour Party that is defending a fundamental principle of democracy and not the government.* (our emphasis)

On 21 September, the day after the by-elections in which Labour retained the seats, Tremlett was sacked from the GLC Conservative Group.

Although the Paving Bill is the most spectacular example of Tory willingness to subvert democracy for political advantage, there are others. In fact, Thatcher's party incubates a whole strain of anti-democratic views. Roger Scruton, editor of the *Salisbury Review* and guru of the far right, claimed in the *Times* (14 February 1984) that local government was unrepresentative and a 'threat to sovereignty' because 'local elections are little understood by those entitled to vote in them and because the taxes levied by the councils come mostly from those who are disenfranchised:

businesses, and central government'.

These views find an echo in the highest reaches of the Tory government. According to the Rates White Paper (Cmnd 9008, August 1983), only about 35 per cent of those eligible to vote in local elections pay full rates, and 'many of those who voted for local spending do not have to make a contribution through the rates'. William Waldegrave has used these assertions to justify the rate-limitation policy: in a party press release of 4 January 1984: 'Parliament has an historic duty to protect the oppressed. This applies now to ratepayers in a minority of councils . . . in these areas there is no proper democratic brake on extortionate councils.'

Yet local government is responsible to its entire electorate and not just to those who pay rates. Everyone over 17 can vote in parliamentary elections, not only those who pay income tax in full. While the government has drawn back from disenfranchising 65 per cent of the local electorate – which the logic of its argument requires – it has given special treatment to the business community. Section 13 of the Rates Act lays a duty on local authorities to consult business ratepayers on their budget proposals – one privilege which no other section of the community enjoys.

Apparently, the government has ruled out the reintroduction of a special business vote – but only on grounds of impractibility. Dealing with a business with several premises in different authorities and weighting votes according to the wealth of the business would, according to the *Sunday Times* (4 November 1984), 'savour too much of plutocracy'.

The abolition of the GLC and the Metropolitan County Councils

■ *We put a firm commitment to abolition in our manifesto. The government has been re-elected with the biggest parliamentary majority since 1945 and we are now firmly committed to this cause.*

Patrick Jenkin MP, Department of the Environment, Press release 393, 21 September 1983

■ *This sad saga is being justified on the ground that the*

proposals were set out in the Conservative Party's manifesto. They were put in nine days after the election was called against the wishes of the party policy committee. They were inserted without the general agreement of those who had been London Conservative Members. The consequences are now apparent for all to see.

Edward Heath MP, *Hansard*, 4 December 1984

The Local Government Bill now in parliament gives effect to the government's proposals to abolish the GLC and metropolitan counties in April 1986. It will transfer the functions of these authorities to a concoction of appointed joint boards, statutory joint committees, *ad hoc* working groups, quangos, central government agencies and, finally, to the metropolitan districts and London boroughs. The Bill is the product of the White Paper *Streamlining the Cities* (Cmnd 9063, October 1983) which was universally criticized in local government and academic circles. The comments of the School of Advanced Urban Studies (*The Future of Local Democracy* November 1983) are typical:

> By any objective judgement the White Paper falls far short of the standards to be expected of a document intended to stimulate and inform public debate on the constitutional, administrative and economic implications of a major change in the structure of government as it operates in the main cities.

The White Paper 'argued' that abolition of the metropolitan upper tier would:

● remove sources of administrative conflict and tension;
● save money;
● provide a simplified system – easier for the public to understand.

In the words of Edward Heath (*Hansard*, 4 December 1984), in the 13 months between the issue of the White Paper and the publication of the Bill, 'no substantial evidence has been produced for abolishing the GLC or the metropolitan counties'. In fact, the arguments for abolition put forward by the main proponents of the Bill – the Environment Secretary,

Patrick Jenkin, and the Local Government Minister, Kenneth Baker – run directly counter to their own earlier views. On 1 August 1977 Jenkin had told the Marshall Inquiry on Greater London:

> I believe we have got progressively to return to the concept that the GLC is a strategic authority . . . the GLC's planning powers should be essentially strategic and provide the framework within which the boroughs should operate the day-to-day planning controls. The GLC should remain responsible for London Transport.

Kenneth Baker, as co-author of the 1977 pamphlet *Maybe It's Because We Are Londoners*, had been equally enthusiastic:

> *The strategic role of the GLC should be enhanced.*
> (our emphasis) In recent years there have been increased direction by central government over local government. Far from the GLC being allowed greater independence Whitehall has, quite wrongly, interfered more and more with the activities of County Hall.

The Bill is costly and will not save money. During the 1983 general election the (then) Minister for Local Government, Tom King MP, claimed that abolition would save at least £120 million a year and that 9,000 jobs would be lost. With the publication of the Local Government Bill, these estimates have been revised downwards to an annual saving of £100 million and a net reduction of 8,000 jobs. But:

● A detailed analysis by management consultants Coopers and Lybrand concluded that abolition of the metropolitan counties was unlikely to produce any net saving and could cost an extra £60 million a year (*Streamlining the Cities*: An Analysis of the Government's Proposals for Reorganizing Local Government, February 1984). In November 1984 the consultants published a further report revising their earlier figures upwards – to £69 million a year.

● For its part, the GLC says the cost of abolishing the council will be £225 million over five years. In addition, the dissolution of the GLC's Capital Fund could add a colossal £1 billion to public sector borrowing over the same period.

● The GLC (including ILEA) and the metropolitan counties (including the police) employ around 155,000 full- and part-time staff. A Department of the Environment press release of 20 September 1984 quotes the Environment Secretary as saying that 'any compulsory redundancies will be relatively few' – yet the government is planning for 8,000 redundancies with compensation totalling £40 million in 1986-7.

The government's claim that abolition will produce savings is credible only if the Environment Secretary uses his powers to reduce service levels (see page 18) to bring them about. These powers are now to be massively extended by the Local Government Bill.

The Bill is undemocratic. The explanatory memorandum to the Bill states that the functions of the GLC and metropolitan counties will be reallocated, respectively, 'principally to the London Borough and met district councils'. In fact, only 18 per cent of current spending in the metropolitan counties will go to the directly elected district councils; in London, only 31 per cent of GLC spending will go to the boroughs. The rest goes to a variety of bodies that are not directly elected – principally to 19 joint boards and 48 joint committees. But it doesn't end there. Lead districts, residual bodies, compulsory and voluntary co-operation and increased powers for central government all feature in the plans. The result is a dramatic loss of accountability.

In the metropolitan districts democratic control of the police, fire services and public transport is to be lost to 18 joint boards consisting of nominated members of the metropolitan districts. In London there will be a joint board for fire and civil defence. Last year, the GLC was stripped of its responsibility for London Transport and control was transferred to a new quango – London Regional Transport (LRT). In addition to the new joint boards, the metropolitan district councils and the London boroughs are expected to co-operate on matters such as waste disposal, planning and traffic management through joint committees.

An analysis of the new joint boards and committees by

academics from the London Business School and the Institute of Local Government Studies warned that, under the proposed system, the electorate would have next to no say in the running of the joint boards. If the electorate did not like the way these services were provided they could not choose to remove board members at an election. The choice of members for these bodies would remain within the local authorities.

The Bill centralizes power. The Secretary of State is to be given sweeping powers to intervene in the operation of the joint boards once established. He can:

● Rate-cap the joint boards, alter their membership and break them up without a prior inquiry. For the first three years of their existence, the precepts and staffing levels of the joint boards will be under direct government control.

● Dismember the Inner London Education Authority at any time and transfer responsibility for education to all or any of the London boroughs.

● Under 'catch-all' Clause 93, the Secretary of State is given draconian powers to amend *any terms* of the Bill after it becomes law, but before abolition. If any part of the legislation proves unworkable – or if the abolition deadline cannot be met – the Secretary of State can simply change it, by order.

Rate-capping

■ *Parliament should recognize that the rate-capping proposals are of constitutional significance, representing a fundamental shift from a dispersal of government power to a massive concentration in central government.*

Professors George Jones and John Stewart,
Guardian, 3 November 1983

The Rates Act 1984 is the most formidable weapon in the Tories' armoury of controls over local government and effectively ends the historic right of local authorities to levy the rates they consider necessary to meet local needs – a right that has existed since 1601. The Act gives the government an unprecedented veto over the financial decisions of all but the smallest and most frugal local authorities. It gives the Secretary of State for the Environment powers to:

- select individual councils which, in his view, are 'spending excessively';
- fix a ceiling on what the selected – or rate-capped – council may raise in rates;
- trigger reserve powers for the imposition of a *general* rate-limitation scheme to control the spending of all authorities other than the very smallest with budgets of £10 million a year or less.

The Rates Act gives the government sweeping powers to fix spending and rates limits, yet cynically leaves councillors with the responsibility for making the inevitable cuts in services. The legislation arises directly from the government's failure to reform the rating system – as promised in two successive Tory manifestos.

The previous Local Government Minister, Tom King MP, had no doubts about the serious constitutional implications of rate-capping. Speaking in the Commons on 18 January 1982, one year after the introduction of the new block-grant system, he made the position absolutely clear:

> It remains the case that while the government still has a responsibility for the distribution of grant, the levels of rates are the responsibility of the local authorities. They have to determine them and remain answerable to their electorate.

The same sentiments had been expressed by the Prime Minister herself at an earlier stage in her career, when addressing the 1965 Conservative Party Conference. Without responsibility for rating, she implied, local government would not amount to very much:

> One must always keep sufficient expenditure with the local authorities; otherwise, the whole basis of local government is undermined for good and all. *The task of a local councillor who was not responsible for rating would be absolutely marvellous.* He could demand everything, the sky would be the limit, and he could blame the

government always if he did not get it. *It would cease to be local government.* (our emphasis)

The pretence that local authorities had to be accountable to their electorates for their own spending decisions was finally jettisoned in 1983. Ministers took refuge in the precedent set by the Local Government (Miscellaneous Provisions) Scotland Act 1981, which gave the government powers to impose selective rate-capping against individual authorities.

Perhaps as a bizarre quirk of the system, no Scottish authority was rate-capped last year. But in the period 1981/2 – 1983/4 seven authorities were ordered to cut their spending.

The government's enthusiasm for rate-capping was not matched on the Tory backbenches – or in Tory local government circles. In fact, rate-capping was seen as nothing less than a threat to the constitution and a departure from traditional Conservatism. The chair of the Tory-controlled Association of County Councillors, John Lovill, told the *Times* on 29 September 1983: 'We are not being disloyal Conservatives. In fact, we are being more faithful to the Conservative philosophy in opposing the White Paper on Rates. The party has lost its way on this issue.' He went on:

The excessive power which central government is proposing will remove from the local voter and ratepayer the right to control their local budgets and determine their local priorities . . . *This would result in the demise of local democracy.* (our emphasis)

The Association of District Councils – also Tory-controlled – was equally forthright. It described the rate-capping proposals as 'a major constitutional change which would be a fundamental breach of local democracy and accountability and be wholly unworkable in practice'.

The Commons second reading of the Rates Bill in January 1984 produced one of the biggest backbench rebellions of this parliament. Five former ministers, including ex-Prime Minister Edward Heath, were among 13 Tories who voted against. Another 20 abstained. A further, but less dramatic, revolt occurred at the Bill's Commons report stage when former Tory Environment Secretary Geoffrey Rippon warned Tory MPs that before supporting the measure they should 'bear in mind that they will be doing so contrary to every precept of the rule of law for which the Conservative Party has ever stood' (*Hansard*, 27 March 1984).

With the arrival of the Rates Act on to the Statute Book the 'rule of law' has little real meaning. The leader and chair of the policy committee on the Tory-controlled Association of County Councils wrote, with some foresight, on 10 October 1983:

> We cannot have councils caught in a vice between statutory rate-capping, and ever-increasing statutory obligations to provide services, and even finding themselves taken to court for non-compliance.

Since then, many councils, and not merely those faced with rate-capping, have pointed to the impossibility of meeting government targets. The experience of Hillingdon – a Tory-controlled Outer London borough – is fairly typical. In 1984–5 the government's assessment of Hillingdon's need to spend was £79.4 million; the authority's budget stood at £87.8 million. The leader of the council told the *Times* on 6 August 1984: 'according to the government, this authority is spending 56 per cent or £5 million above their [social services] assessment. To cut expenditure to the government's assessment is *impossible*.'

Public spending cuts

Tory constraints on local spending

Since taking office in 1979, the Tories have armed themselves with a battery of financial and legal controls to curb the activities of elected local authorities and to force massive cuts in jobs and services.

Councils' capital expenditure on house-building, modernization programmes and in other key areas such as roads and schools has always been tightly constrained by central government. But the Tories have slashed capital spending in both central and local government services. Between 1979–80 and 1984–5 local authority capital expenditure has been cut by over 60 per cent in real terms. In 1985–6, the government plans to cut a further £1 billion from councils' capital spending. This amounts to a 20 per cent reduction on last year and is equivalent to signing redundancy notices for about 150,000 construction workers.

On current expenditure – wages, salaries and other running costs of services – local authorities, except those designated under the Rates Act (see page 26) are, theoretically, free to finance whatever level of spending they decide upon. For this they use their own source of locally controlled taxation – the rates – topped up by central government grants. The Tories have intensified their attack on local current expenditure by cutting central government grants, forcing councils to choose between massive cuts in services or punitive rate rises. Over the six years from 1979–80 to 1985–6 the real value of Exchequer grants to local authorities has been cut by 12.3 per cent – an accumulated loss over the period of nearly £8.5 billion.

In 1979/80 Exchequer grants were 61 per cent of total local authority spending. In 1985–6, they will drop below half of total spending for *the first time ever*. The grant – at £11.8 billion – represents a massive £775 million cut in real terms over the previous year. Overall, the total provision for local authorities' current expenditure in 1985–6 is £21.3 billion – or £1.1 billion less than local authorities say they need simply *to maintain* existing levels of service. Last year, a group of officials from local and central government, reporting to the Consultative Council on Local Government Finance (a body which brings together ministers and representatives of local government), estimated that a cut of over £1 billion, amounting to 5 per cent in real terms, could mean:

● **Savage reductions in staffing levels, including:**

Teachers	45,000
Police service	10,200
Fire service	2,400
Public transport	3,550

- **Reductions in service levels for Personal Social Services, including:**

Loss of residential places for:	
The elderly	5,800
Mentally handicapped	800
Children	1,500
Loss of day-care places:	
Day nurseries	1,500
Day centres for the elderly	1,500
Adult training centres	2,300
Other day care	1,000
Loss of community services:	
Home helps (homes attended)	35,000
Meals (per week)	40,000
Boarded-out children	1,800

Central government grants have been cut but, overall, the Tories have made the heaviest cuts in some of the hard-pressed inner cities: areas where the needs are greatest and where Labour-controlled local authorities are making great efforts to maintain the standards of local services. The Inner London Education Authority is among those councils which have lost all their Rate Support Grant entitlement through the operation of grant penalties (see page 23).

Since 1980 Tory ministers have been compiling 'hit lists' of local authorities, to be subjected to special cuts in grants as a penalty for 'overspending'. From 1981 the Tories recast the structure of the Rate Support Grant (RSG), which is the main Exchequer grant to local authorities, in England and Wales. Under the terms of the Local Government Planning and Land Act 1980, each local authority was for the first time told by central government exactly how much ministers thought the council ought to be spending. There is an automatic penalty built into the RSG so that those authorities spending more than a specified 'threshold' level get proportionately less grant.

Since 1981 in England, and since 1982 in Wales, each

local authority has been faced with *two completely contradictory targets* imposed by ministers for the level of current expenditure. These are:

● The Grant Related Expenditure Assessment (GREA), used to determine the basic RSG entitlement. This is a supposedly objective assessment of what an authority ought to be spending on its services, having regard to its population and certain factors of social need. However, the needs assessments are very crude, and some deprived inner-city areas are assessed at a lower GREA per head of population compared with much less needy areas elsewhere.

● The penalty target, used to determine special RSG penalties for a council deemed to be overspending. This target takes account of the council's actual expenditure level in recent years. It is designed to ensure a sharp reduction in expenditure from year to year if special penalties are to be avoided.

Table 1 shows how penalties affected authorities at different levels of spending above target.

Table 1

Year	1%	2%	3%	4%	5%	10%	20%
1983–4	1p	2p	7p	12p	17p	42p	92p
1984–5	2p	6p	14p	23p	32p	77p	167p
1985–6	7p	15p	24p	33p	42p	87p	177p

The figures mean that in the current year (1985–6) an authority spending 10 per cent above the government's target will lose grant equivalent to 87p on the rates.

Even the government's own watchdog on local government finance – the Audit Commission – has severely criticized the block-grant system. In a report published in August 1984, the commission claimed that:

● Government policies have been responsible for rates £1.2 billion higher than they might otherwise have been without the uncertainties of the block-grant system.

- Expenditure targets and penalties should be abolished 'as soon as practically possible'.
- The complexities of the system inhibit authorities from planning ahead.

The Audit Commission's chief officer, John Banham, has called for 'a root and branch review of the present [grant system] arrangements'.

The trend of spending and rates

Allowing for the huge cuts in capital spending, local authorities' local expenditure (current and capital) has fallen substantially – even while central government's own expenditure has been increasing in total. As a percentage of total public spending (central and local) the local authorities' share has fallen from over 28 per cent in 1979–80 to 25 per cent in 1984–5.

Local rates have been forced up considerably under the Tory government. In national terms, all the increases can be attributed to cuts in grant. Over the five years up to 1983–4, household rates rose by nearly 130 per cent – or by 33 per cent after allowing for inflation. However, cuts in Exchequer grants would have forced rates up by 37 per cent (over and above inflation) if councils' spending in real terms had stood still. The actual trend of council expenditure, before allowing for inflation and cuts in government grants, would have allowed rates *to fall* by 2.5 per cent.

As part of their overall economic policy, the Tories have shifted the burden of financing local authority expenditure away from the taxpayer and on to the ratepayer. To restore the RSG to the level the Tories inherited when they came to office would cost the Exchequer £3 billion.

The result of a transfer of this magnitude back into local government would be dramatic. The Local Government Campaign Unit has estimated (29 November 1984) that if grant were restored to 1979 levels, weekly domestic rate bills could go down by between:

- £2.22 and £6.31 in Inner London;

- £1.71 (35 per cent) and £2.52 (48 per cent) in metropolitan districts within a county such as Tyne and Wear;
- £1 (13 per cent) and £1.86 (20 per cent) in shire districts within a county such as Surrey.

As part of its drive to release labour and other resources for the private sector, the government has pressed local authorities to cut back on the number of workers they employ. Spiralling unemployment throughout the whole economy has done little to dent Tory enthusiasm for this objective.

In the three and a half years from June 1979 to December 1983 the total number of local government employees fell by nearly 100,000, or by 5.5 per cent. But, ironically, over the same period, councils took on 15,581 employees (or 1 per cent) to deal with extra responsibilities heaped on local authorities by the government. The Local Authorities' Conditions of Service Advisory Board has estimated that these 'central government initiatives' have cost councils £128 million over this period (*Effects of Central Government Initiatives on Local Government*, October 1984). To take one example, in Berkshire – where the Tories have a majority but no overall control – these initiatives cost the council £750,000 in 1983. The chief executive complained in a letter to the *Times* (8 September 1983) that the county had had to take on 50 extra staff to handle new duties placed on the council.

However, in those services favoured by the government, the numbers employed have increased dramatically. 'Law and order' staff (police, probation and magistrates' staff) went up by 14,500 over the period. In other areas, though, there have been deep cuts:

- 72,000 fewer staff in education, including 27,000 fewer teachers;
- 16,000 fewer building workers;
- 12,200 fewer staff in social services;
- 4,700 fewer employed in engineering;
- 5,500 fewer in leisure and recreation services.

The effect of the Rates Act

■ *We have been legislated into a corner.*

Roger Parker-Jervis, resigning as Chair of
Buckinghamshire County Council, *Times*,
8 November 1984

On 24 July 1984, the Secretary of State for the Environment
announced the first batch of councils to be rate-capped. All
but two (Brent and Portsmouth) of the 18 councils are
Labour-controlled and were spending 4 per cent or more over
target and 20 per cent or more above the government's
allegedly objective assessment of their spending needs
(GREA).

The Secretary of State ordered 15 of the designated
authorities to freeze their spending for 1985–6 at the 1984–5
level – with no provision for inflation. The GLC, ILEA and
Greenwich were set expenditure limits 1.5 per cent below
their 1984–5 budgets.

The Association of Metropolitan Authorities has calculated that the cuts required, far from simply pegging
spending, amount to a reduction of nearly 12 per cent, in real
terms.

Thirteen authorities have been ordered to decrease their
rates:

	% rate decrease
Leicester	−56.61
Southwark	−24.74
Lewisham	−24.41
Greenwich	−18.91
Lambeth	−12.07
Islington	− 9.39
ILEA	− 7.26
Hackney	− 4.37
Haringey	− 3.05
S. Yorkshire	− 2.39
Portsmouth	−1.18
Sheffield	− 0.56
GLC	− 0.08

The remaining five have been given limits higher than current rates or precepts. These are:

	% rate increase
Camden	+ 0.09
Brent	+ 1.55
Thamesdown	+ 5.59
Basildon	+17.59
Merseyside	+27.48

The Secretary of State has refused to disclose the detailed assumptions which might explain his decisions on the rate levels of individual authorities. But some – such as Leicester – will clearly be forced to plunder their own balances to preserve services.

The Tories have turned to rate controls because of their failure to achieve *total* control of local authority expenditure purely by manipulating grants. A few authorities have exhausted their RSG entitlement altogether as a result of the grant penalties, and can be threatened by no further loss of grant. But the logic of rate-capping is such that more and more councils are likely to be ensnared.

What rate-capping will mean for services

■ *Don't let anyone tell that rate-capping means inevitable cuts in services. That's nonsense.*

Lord Bellwin, then Minister of State,
Department of the Environment press notice 94,
21 February 1984

■ *Most of the high-spending authorities can achieve the savings that we seek without dramatic or unduly painful cuts.*

Patrick Jenkin MP, 7 November 1984

The 18 rate-capped councils in England face crippling cuts in services if they are to meet government spending limits. Evidence from the 'hit list' authorities confirms that, in real terms, the cuts demanded are nearly 12 per cent. The prospects of cuts in services of this size are chilling.

Table 2

| | Cuts required | |
	£m	%
Hackney	−35.7	−30.2
Merseyside	−44.3	−17.8
Leicester	− 5.6	−18.7
Greenwich	−11.7	−15.0
Lewisham	−13.7	−14.7
S. Yorkshire	−27.7	−13.5
Haringey	−19.8	−13.4
Thamesdown	− 1.7	−10.6
Brent	−34.0	−19.5
Sheffield	−32.4	−13.0
Southwark	−22.6	−17.2
Camden	−15.9	−11.9
Lambeth	−17.9	−13.6
Basildon	− 1.4	− 9.2
Islington	− 8.5	− 9.0
ILEA	−57.0	− 6.0
Portsmouth	− 1.3	− 7.6
GLC	−74.8	− 8.7

Table 2 shows the cuts required to meet the government's expenditure limits. Southwark faces the impossible task of cutting its spending next year by over 17 per cent – or £22.6 million. If the cuts were made on a pro rata basis over all services, there would, for example, have to be a reduction of £5.4 million in social services. Leading to:

● the closure of seven residential homes for children;
● the closure of five old people's homes;
● the closure of all the day centres for the mentally ill;
● a 21 per cent cut in the number of social workers;
● the ending of all grants to voluntary organizations working with the vulnerable and needy.

According to estimates from ILEA, keeping within the government's target could mean:

Table 3   Spending on local authority services (England) 1984–5

	£ spent per head of population	As % of total spending
Education	251.80	48.2
Police	54.76	10.5
Personal social services	50.63	9.7
Highways	32.55	6.2
Housing	24.07	4.6
Passenger transport	17.15	3.3
Refuse	13.45	2.6
Fire	12.09	2.3
Town and country planning	9.49	1.8
Libraries, museums and art galleries	8.84	1.7
Parks and open spaces	8.59	1.6
Environmental health	7.32	1.4
Swimming pools and sports centres, etc.	6.88	1.3
All other services	24.73	4.7
Total	**522.35**	**100.0**

Note: Figures show spending net of income from rents, charges, and grant income.
Source: Finance and General Statistics 1984–5, CIPFA, May 1984.

● the loss of over 5,000 teaching and non–teaching jobs;
● a 30 per cent cut in the cash allowances to schools for books, equipment and stationery;
● a 43 per cent increase in school meals prices;
● major cuts in adult education classes and soaring fees.

And this is against a background where one–quarter of ILEA's pupils come from one–parent families (two–thirds higher than the national average) and over one–third of children qualify for free school meals – twice the national average.

The GLC has calculated that a £74.8 million budget cut would mean:

- the loss of 500 fire brigade jobs and fewer appliances;
- the loss of funding for over 100 community groups currently supported by the women's, police and ethnic minorities committees;
- the end of the pioneering 'dial–a–ride' scheme for disabled people;
- drastic cuts in the Stress Boroughs Programme which channels resources to London's most deprived boroughs.

What local authorities spend their money on
Table 3 shows how the total cost of local government breaks down between the main spending services.

Health

'*The NHS is safe with us*' has been the rallying cry of successive Tory Party Conferences. But if the NHS is safe with Margaret Thatcher why does Margaret Thatcher not feel safe with the NHS?

In 1982 she jumped the queue for a varicose vein operation and went to the private Fitzroy Nuffield Hospital. In 1983 she required an operation for a detached retina, for which there is no NHS waiting list. She chose to go to the private Princess Christian Hospital – which didn't have the right equipment for the operation and had to borrow it from the NHS King Edward VII Hospital down the road.

Thatcher's behaviour is but a reflection of the new Tories' contempt for the NHS and the principles on which it was founded – that good quality health care should be available to all on the basis of medical need and irrespective of the ability to pay.

The Tories are undermining the NHS from all sides. They are proceeding step by step towards a two–tier health service – a growing commercial sector for the wealthy and healthy and a deprived, demoralized public service for the rest.

NHS spending

■ *In the five years to 1983–4, expenditure on the NHS has doubled, representing an increase of some 17 per cent measured against the Retail Price Index and providing for significant real growth in services after allowing for the extra costs facing the NHS.*

Public Expenditure White Paper, February 1984

The government has exploited the complexities of health service finance to mislead the public over its commitment to the NHS. It has consistently claimed to be spending more than ever on the NHS. What the government fails to tell us is that spending needs to rise every year just for services to stand still. In fact, government spending on the NHS has failed to keep pace with the increased demands made on the service.

In order to assess the government's record on NHS spending, it is important to unravel some of the features of health service finance.

Inflation allowances. The Retail Price Index is not an appropriate guide to the movement in prices within the NHS. It is officially recognized that prices in the NHS have risen by an average of 1.5 percentage points more than the general rise in prices each year for the past five years.

Demographic change. The rise in the number of very elderly people places increasing demands on the NHS. On average it costs the NHS almost nine times as much to care for someone over 75 as for someone of working age. It has been officially estimated that over most of the period since 1979 growth of 0.7 per cent each year was required to meet the demands of demographic change. More recently, the estimate has been revised upward to 1 per cent growth.

Technological change. Advances in medical science have led to the introduction of new diagnostic and treatment techniques, often involving expensive equipment and making greater demands on staff time. The DHSS calculates that

31

growth of 0.5 per cent each year is needed simply to keep abreast of such innovations.

Redistribution. The government's national budget for the NHS is not distributed evenly throughout the country. Resources are distributed to the regional health authorities according to a formula devised by the Resources Allocation Working Party (RAWP) to overcome long-standing regional disparities in NHS provision. Thus, although the government claims a 1 per cent growth in the 1984–5 budget, the spread of regional allocations is from 1.9 per cent growth for East Anglia to nil growth in the four Thames regions. Redistribution is a desirable goal. But in periods of nil or low growth nationally, it inevitably involves major cuts for certain regions.

Different services. The NHS is not a single service. There are two main elements within the NHS budget. One is an allocation to health authorities to fund hospitals and community health services, such as home nursing, health visiting, chiropody, family planning clinics. This represents about 70 per cent of the total budget. The other is payments to family practitioners, such as GPs, dentists, opticians and pharmacists. Health authorities are obliged by law to remain within the cash sums allocated by the government for funding their services. By contrast, the government has little direct control over the budget of family practitioner services – this is largely determined by the level of public demand on the services.

The first five years of Tory power

Taking all these factors into account, the true picture of government spending on the NHS looks very different from ministerial claims. Instead of the 17 per cent increase claimed by the government in the five years since 1979:

● Real growth in the NHS budget overall was just over 7 per cent.

● Real growth in resources to health authorities was just 4 per cent. But resources needed to increase by 6 to 6.5 per cent in real terms for the same level of service to be maintained. Thus, the health authority budgets were *cut* by 2 to 2.5 per cent over the five-year period.

● Real growth in resources to family practitioner services was 9 per cent.

The 1984–5 budget

For 1984–5 the government allocated an extra £800 million for the NHS in Great Britain – real growth in resources of 1 per cent, it claimed. But this claim, like its others, is utterly misleading. The health budget was cut again.

● In August 1983 health authority budgets were cut by 1 per cent as part of the Lawson package of public expenditure cuts. As the 1984 House of Commons Social Services Committee pointed out: 'To cut 1 per cent in one year and restore it in the next year is not "growth".'

● 1.5 per cent growth is in any event required each year to keep up with demographic and technological pressures.

● Health authorities have had to find a further £48 million out of their reduced budget to meet that part of the health workers' pay settlement the government refused to fund.

For the future, the government claims, 'the plans provide for growth in resources of about 1 per cent over each of the next three years'. But this 1 per cent growth, already inadequate to keep up with rising demands, depends upon pay and prices in the NHS being below the general rise in prices in the economy – something that has never happened in the past. The outlook is clear – services in the NHS will continue to deteriorate.

Family practitioner services

Having established tight controls over health authority budgets, the government is now turning its attention to family practitioner services. In 1983 Norman Fowler, at the behest of the Treasury, asked Binder Hamlyn, a firm of City accountants, to see how expenditure on these services could be contained. Their report made a number of recommendations for cutting costs – including controls over staff numbers. The government has found the report politically embarrassing and has refused to publish it. Now it plans to issue a Green Paper on primary care early in 1985 which will undoubtedly include proposals for restraining family practitioner spending.

Staff cuts

In 1983, for the first time ever, the government insisted on staff cuts, in addition to cash cuts. Health authorities were ordered to cut staffing levels by nearly 5,000 from their 31 March 1983 level. In the event, health authorities cut 11,400 jobs in 1983–4, including 3,100 nursing jobs. For 1984–5, the government has demanded that health authorities stay within the staffing levels set the previous year. Since the previous year's staff cuts were greater than the government's guidelines, most regions will be able to take on staff – provided they can pay for them. But three of the Thames regions have been told that they can employ no more staff and the North-east Thames region has been told to cut staff by a further 300.

Staff cuts have been made while unemployment among doctors and nurses is rising. The Tories stopped collecting unemployment statistics according to occupation in September 1982. But:

● between September 1979 and September 1982 unemployment among qualified nurses and midwives more than doubled – from just over 4,000 to nearly 9,000;
● between September 1980 and September 1982 unemployment among doctors trebled from 493 to 1,418.

Since then, we can only estimate the level of medical unemployment. But a 1983 British Medical Association (BMA) survey of junior hospital doctors found that at least 700 were unemployed at any one time, and that one in five junior doctors had been unemployed at some time in the previous two years.

The government defends its record on the NHS by showing that despite these staff and cash cuts, more patients are being treated that ever before. But these figures don't show what quality of care patients are receiving; nor do they show the extra strains placed upon health workers, family practitioners, social services and families by the quicker through-put of patients.

The effect on services
In contrast to the government's misleading claims, the views of those who work in the health service show what is really happening.

● A 1983 survey by the Royal College of Nursing (RCN) reported extremely low levels of nursing on the wards: 'Nurses want the public to know that standards of care are already threatened, that staffing levels on wards hover just above danger level and that out in the community increased numbers of patients are over-burdening community care and making good nursing practice practically impossible.'

● A survey by the BMA found that in 1983 waiting times for hospital appointments had increased by an average of 20 per cent over the previous year.

● In a letter to the *Times* (21 March 1984) the presidents of the Royal Colleges warned: 'Without adequate funding the future development of preventive medicine, health care and improvements from advances in medicine will be threatened.'

● A report by the Standing Medical Advisory Committee (October 1984) found that the constraints on resources 'have particularly significant implications for services to cancer patients . . . The gap between the level of services generally available and the level that it is now possible to achieve has increased considerably.'

● Screening for cervical cancer has been badly hit by lack of funds. The government closed the national recall system in 1980 and passed responsibility for establishing an effective screening and recall system to the 98 family practitioner committees in England and Wales. But by April 1984 only 27 had fully computerized systems; 13 others had limited computer records. The majority of committees have no plans for systematic screening systems – leaving millions of women at risk.

● The British Kidney Patients' Association estimate that 3,000 kidney patients die each year because of the lack of treatment. Just £50 million would pay for the 50 badly needed units.

Drug costs

The government came under pressure to cut drug company profits after the Public Accounts Committee report in March 1983 found:

● In recent years drug company profits had been 5 to 10 per cent higher than levels reached in industry generally.
● In 1979 and 1980 the larger pharmaceutical companies made profits of over £33 million more than is allowed under the Pharmaceutical Price Regulation Scheme (PPRS), of which less than £3 million was clawed back by the DHSS.

In August 1983 the government reduced drug industry profits by £25 million as part of the Lawson cuts. Despite this, the drug companies made a profit of £200 million on their UK sales in 1983. From April 1984, the government renegotiated the PPRS:

● drug company profit rates were reduced from 25 to 21 per cent;
● the amount of promotional spending allowed was cut by 1 per cent;
● the price freeze agreed in 1983 was to continue.

The government claims that this package will save the NHS £65 million in 1984–5, rising to over £100 million in future years. However, a *Guardian* survey (July 1984) found that despite the freeze, price rises had been allowed for at least 21 firms since April. It seems that the 12 people at the DHSS who administer the PPRS are no match for multinationals' company accountants. No wonder Norman Fowler was able to claim that 'Although the industry sees the new PPRS as tough . . . it is something they can live with.'

The government is also treading more softly than it seeks to claim over limiting the NHS drugs bill. It has rejected the Greenfield Report's recommendations for widespread generic substitution which would save up to 10 per cent of the £2,000 million NHS drugs bill. Instead, it has introduced limited reforms which combine the worst of all worlds. From April 1985 doctors will be required to prescribe generic drugs for conditions such as coughs and colds and for tranquillizers and sedatives. The proposals will introduce a two-tier service into general practice – those who can afford a private prescription will still be able to obtain their favourite drug. Norman Fowler optimistically claimed the limited list could save the NHS £100 million a year – but this money is not being ploughed back into the service. In 1985–6, government plans project a fall in expenditure on family practitioner services.

Charges
Health charges have increased astronomically under the Tories, completely undermining the principle of a health service free at the point of use.

● **Prescription charges** have risen from 20p in May 1979 to £1.60 in April 1984. In April 1985 they will rise again to at least £1.80 – an increase of over 14 per cent, three times the rate of inflation.

● The maximum charge for routine **dental treatment** has gone up from £5 in May 1979 to £14.50 in April 1984; for more complicated treatment, from £30 to £110. It will rise again in April 1985.

● **Optical charges** have also been increased. Maximum charges for lenses have risen from £6.15 in May 1979 to £16.50 in April 1984.

● In 1978–9 charges met 6.5 per cent of the cost of **family practitioner services.** Now they meet 11.5 per cent of the cost.

● In October 1982, the government introduced a new charge – **overseas visitors** not covered by a reciprocal health agreement had to pay for a stay in hospital. The scheme has proved a fiasco. It was expected to raise £6 million a year. In the first six months it had raised under £400,000. It has, however, led to the harassment of black British residents and imposed an extra burden on already overworked staff.

Glasses privatized

From April 1985, the general supply of NHS glasses (lenses and frames) will end.

NHS glasses will be available only to children under 16 and families in receipt of supplementary benefit, family income supplement or otherwise on low incomes. For adults, NHS glasses will become a visible badge of poverty.

Everyone else, including elderly people not on supplementary pension, will have to buy their glasses privately. Those people who used to have NHS glasses will have to pay more for them. And those with the worst eyesight will pay the most.

Non-opticians are now able to dispense glasses against a prescription following a sight test by a qualified optician. The restrictions on advertising have also been reduced. The Association of Optical Productions has warned that this could lead to the demise of many small dispensers in rural areas.

The government is dismantling a vital part of the NHS and turning it over to the private sector. For the paltry saving of £17 million.

Organizational madness

In 1982, the Tories reorganized the NHS, undoing some of the damage done through their original reorganization in the early 1970s. But they also did away with many of the democratic features introduced by the last Labour government. They:

● **reduced local authority representation** on health authorities from a third to a quarter;

● **cut representation of health service workers** on health authorities and encouraged health authorities to seek nominations from non-TUC-affiliated unions;

● **cut Community Health Councils in size,** withdrew the government grant from *CHC News* and questioned the future of the councils.

Barely two years after that reorganization, the government

instituted a further management shake-up of the NHS. The Secretary of State appointed Roy Griffiths, managing director of Sainsbury's, to investigate the management of the NHS. His brief report in autumn 1983 recommended:

● the establishment of a Health Service Supervisory Board and an NHS Management Board within the DHSS;
● an enhanced role for chairs of health authority, who are appointed by the Secretary of State;
● the identification of a general manager at every level of the NHS who would have responsibility for final decision-taking and for identifying 'cost-improvement programmes'.

The report's recommendations reduce the scope for local decision-taking by health authority members, overturn the concept of consensus management and enhance the power of the Secretary of State to impose cost-cutting exercises on the NHS. Despite professional opposition and a critical report from the House of Commons Social Services Committee, Norman Fowler has pushed ahead with implementing the report – although not as fast as he would have liked. A year elapsed after the report's publication before the government could find someone to chair the NHS Management Board. And implementation of the report by the health authorities looks increasingly like a policy of 'jobs for the boys'. By October 1984, 10 of the 14 English regional health authorities had appointed general managers from among their existing top managers – at an extra £3,000 each per annum.

Health service for sale
During Thatcher's first administration, the government made several attempts to encourage health authorities to contract out their ancillary services to commercial contractors. But health authorities largely ignored these moves.

● Between 1979 and 1982 the proportion of services contracted out by health authorities fell: privatized laundry services were 15 per cent of total expenditure in 1978–9, but only 12 per cent in 1981–2; in cleaning, the share fell from 2.4 per cent to 2.1 per cent; and catering stayed constant at 0.2 per cent.

Since the 1983 election, the government has stepped up the pressure on health authorities to 'privatize'. In September 1983, a circular was sent to all district health authorities requiring them to draw up timetables for putting their catering, cleaning and laundry services out to competitive tender and to award contracts to the lowest bidder.

In February 1983, the government claimed that 'privatization' could save £20 million a year on the £800 million spent by the NHS on these three services. But the basis of that assumption was a DHSS study on the unrepresentative experience of military hospitals contracting out cleaning services in 1981. The government's arguments of greater efficiency and economy are a smokescreen for its dogmatic commitment to private enterprise and its desire to line the pockets of business friends. The government has forced its privatization plans on reluctant health authorities – the message is clear: 'Privatize, whatever the costs.' Standards, patients and workers are the victims of doctrinaire policy:

● Health ministers rejected an offer by laundry workers in Cornwall to save the health authority up to £500,000 a year through cuts in their bonus payments; instead, they forced the authority to award its linen contract to Kneels, a subsidiary of Johnson Group cleaners, at an extra cost of £50,000 a year.

● Quality-control checks on a private laundry used by a Cheltenham hospital found that 73 per cent of sheets and 85 per cent of pillowcases failed to meet NHS standards of cleanliness.

● Dr William Newson, a bacteriologist, complained of high levels of dust in clinical areas after the cleaning contract had been awarded to private contractors at Hinchingbroke Hospital: 'We grew coagulese positive staphylococii [potential disease-producers] from three samples of dust in the nursery and Rowan Ward,' his report stated.

● The cleaning firm Crothalls cut the take-home pay of its workers up by to 30 per cent in order to reduce its tender price from £367,000 to £211,000 for cleaning at Barking Hospital.

Opposition to the government's privatization programme

has come from all quarters:

● Trust House Forte has withdrawn from its NHS catering contracts and has told the DHSS it will not be tendering for more because the terms laid down by ministers are dangerous to patients and damaging to staff. 'It's easy to put in bids at a low price,' said Ron Forte, the group's chief executive, 'but what sort of service could we provide?' Gary Hawles, managing director of their catering division, said: 'I have no desire to appear in the media accused of exploiting patients.' (*Sunday Times*, 23 September 1984).

● In October 1984, Mr John Davis, a consultant paediatrician and professor of paediatrics at Cambridge University resigned from his post at Addenbrooke's Hospital where industrial action had been taken as a result of the cleaning contract being awarded to Office Cleaning Services. He said he would not be associated with government-enforced contracting-out which resulted in the loss of loyal and valued staff, interfered with standards of hospital care and reduced ancillary workers to the status of service–casual labour: 'If we are not prepared to pay the economic price for acting morally we may end up by paying the moral price for acting economically,' he commented.

Private practice

■ *Conservatives reject Labour's contention that the state can and should do everything. We welcome the growth in private health insurance in recent years . . . We shall continue to encourage this valuable supplement to state care.*

Conservative manifesto, June 1983

During Thatcher's first administration, the Tories introduced a series of measures to encourage the development of private practice. They:

● scrapped Labour's Health Services Board, which had supervised the removal of pay beds from the NHS;
● relaxed the controls on the development of private hospitals outside the NHS;
● encouraged health authorities to use the private sector, and lifted the ban on contractual arrangements between the NHS

and the profit-making private sector;

● gave tax relief on employers' contributions to private health insurance for lower-paid employees;

● renegotiated consultants' contracts, so that they could do private work without loss of their NHS salary;

● circulated their civil servants with offers of private health insurance at specially discounted rates.

In this favourable climate, the private sector grew apace:

● In 1980 the number of subscribers to the three main provident associations – BUPA, PPP and WPA – grew by 27.5 per cet, and in 1981 by 13.1 per cent. Since then, the growth in subscribers has dropped dramatically – in 1982 it was only 2.9 per cent – as the provident associations have had to raise premiums sharply in order to meet escalating private health care costs. But there are now around 4.5 million people covered by private health insurance, compared to less than 2.5 million at the end of 1978.

● There are 178 private hospitals in England, providing acute care in 7,700 beds; five in Scotland, with 500 beds; and five in Wales, with 200 beds. Proposals to provide a further 1,084 beds in England were lodged with the DHSS in 1983 alone.

Now the government is considering plans to take account of the availability of private facilities when allocating resources to health authorities. In a speech to the Royal Institute for Public Administration in June 1984, Kenneth Clarke, Minister for Health, complained that NHS budget allocations were made as though the private sector did not exist: 'Health authorities should collaborate with the private sector to avoid wasteful duplication of facilities,' he said.

But private practice can only survive as a parasite on the NHS:

● Private health insurance rarely covers childbirth or care for the elderly, mentally ill and mentally handicapped – all the services which cost the NHS so much.

● It relies on the NHS for trained staff. It costs the taxpayer about £100,000 to train a doctor.

● The NHS provides a back-up when things go wrong. A

survey by the organization NHS Unlimited found that less than a third of England's private hospitals had a resident doctor.

Inequalities in health

While the health of the nation has improved during the 35 years of the NHS's existence, marked inequalities in health still exist between the social classes. The Black Report of 1980 revealed that:

● Babies born to unskilled manual workers are twice as likely to die at birth or in the first month of life as babies born to professional-class parents; the sons of unskilled manual workers are five times, and daughters four times, as likely to die in the following 11 months as children of professional-class parents.

● These inequalities are reflected throughout life. For every man from the professional classes who dies from a respiratory disease, six unskilled manual workers die.

The working group which produced the report argued that much of the reason for these inequalities could be found in factors such as work, or the lack of it, the environment, education, housing, living standards, transport. The government gave the report short shrift.

Just 260 copies were printed initially and no press conference was given. Patrick Jenkin, then Secretary of State for Social Services, refused to endorse the report's recommendations and said the additional expenditure required to implement them was 'quite unrealistic in the present or any foreseeable circumstances'.

Since 1979 and the advent of Thatcherism, Britain has seen:

● a massive increase in unemployment;
● unprecedented levels of poverty;
● a rise in homelessness;
● a fall in housing standards;
● environmental decline.

These factors will serve only to increase inequalities in health.

Privatization: the cut-price threat to services

■ *Local authority after local authority has found that even the prospect of contracting out their refuse collection produced amazing economies from their staff. Where Wandsworth Council has led, let other Conservative councils follow.*

> Margaret Thatcher, 1982 Conservative Party Conference

In the first six months of street cleaning in Wandsworth, Pritchards, the private contractors concerned, were 'fined' £7,665 for work below authorized cleaning standards. They have also been fired from their five-year garden maintenance contract in Wandsworth, having accumulated £138,000 in 'fines' within a year.

Whatever the service, privatization has meant poorer quality and higher overall costs in the long run. *Contractors' Failures*, a TUC report on privatization published in November 1984, cited the following examples of poor service.

NHS cleaning. Redbridge Community Health Council conducted a report into the standards of service provided by Crothalls, a subsidiary of Pritchards. In the kitchens, the report found 'a thick layer of grease and dirt under the utensil sink and the presence of dead and decomposing cockroaches indicates the lack of regular and effective cleaning. Several live cockroaches were also seen.'

NHS laundry. Sunlight Laundry hold the contract for Cheltenham District Health Authority. Tests in September 1983 found that only 15 per cent of pillowcases met NHS quality-control standards; the DHSS's recommended acceptance level is 95 per cent. With sheets, 73 per cent were rejected.

Refuse collection. Seventy-nine authorities – of which 48 were Conservative-controlled – had considered and turned down private contractors, according to a recent survey (*Local Government Chronicle*, 17 June 1984). A report by the Audit Commission (August 1984) also concluded that private refuse collection is not cheaper.

In South Oxfordshire, refuse collection is undertaken by Pritchards. In July 1984 a local paper reported a resident's complaints of 'rats breeding in the contractor's dustcart depot', 'horrible smells', and dustcarts left loaded over the weekend with 'rubbish that could become combustible and set on fire'.

School cleaning. In Dudley, school cleaning is carried out by Taskmasters Office Cleaning Services and Initial Cleaning Services. A report by the local branch of the National Union of Teachers complained of 'dirty sinks in lavatories, lack of dusting and polishing, and debris in craft rooms not swept up'. It added: 'a permanent smog-like atmosphere of dust and toilet smells lingers in the corridors.'

School meals. Merton Council has contracted this service out to Sutcliffe. Take-up has fallen by one-fifth. A report by local trade unionists remarked that 'Chips are served quite regularly; there are rarely more than a dozen chips, which are very small and soggy – almost inedible.'

General services. Merton Council boasts that it is the first 'local authority to privatize meals for the elderly and needy'. In local press reports on meals-on-wheels, one home help with six years' experience commented: 'I've never seen anything quite so bad in all my years of service. One old woman was almost in tears and I had to throw it away and make her something else.'

Wages and conditions have suffered, as well as services:

● The hourly wage rate paid to school cleaners in Birmingham by private contractors International Servis System has been cut by over 20 per cent, to £1.71, compared with £2.24 under direct labour. The number of holidays has been cut from 23–25 days to 20. No sick pay is given now. There is no longer a superannuation scheme available.

● In Wirral, Waste Management Limited (a subsidiary of National Freight Consortium) expect workers to shift three tonnes of rubbish from 275 bins a day while walking 17 miles at an average of 3.7 miles an hour.

Personal social services

Local authority social services care for the most vulnerable in our society – disadvantaged children, elderly people, those suffering from mental illness and people with handicaps. But they have been shown no mercy by Thatcher's government. Overall spending on the Personal Social Services has risen by 12.7 per cent in real terms between 1978–9 and 1983–4. The government claims that this is evidence of its concern to protect the weakest. But this limited growth (in the previous ten years social services spending rose by 150 per cent in real terms) has been achieved by local authorities *in spite of*, not because of, government policies. Many local authorities have attempted to protect services to those most in need in the face of continuing government pressure on their expenditure. But although spending on the Personal Social Services has been rising, it has not been sufficient to keep up with demand.

Rising demand

The government itself admits that a 2 per cent growth is needed each year just to keep pace with the increasing number of very elderly people and factors such as the increasing number of difficult children in care. Independent observers suggest this is an underestimate. Rising unemployment and the accompanying increase in poverty and family tensions, cuts in other services and the government's own policies, have all added to the pressures on social services departments.

● A survey in one local authority showed that 4 per cent of families in full-time employment sought help from the local social services department, but 29 per cent of families where the male wage-earner was out of work turned to the same department for urgent advice.

● Between 1981 and 1983 there was a 33 per cent plus increase in Section 1 payments, made by social service departments to help families in difficulty and prevent children being taken into care.

● Financial restraint in the health service, which has led to a

46

faster through-put of patients, has placed extra demands on social services departments to provide home helps, meals-on-wheels, etc.

● Government legislation such as the Criminal Justice Act and the Mental Health Act has given departments new responsibilities without any extra resources. The government's professed policy of 'community care' also means that social services departments should be providing more services for elderly, mentally handicapped and mentally ill people in order either to prevent their reception into institutions or to assist people back into the community.

The Association of Directors of Social Services suggests that 4–6 per cent annual growth is necessary in order for services to stand still. In its survey of local social services departments published in December 1983, the association concluded that 'since 1979 the resources of the Personal Social Services have probably fallen 10 per cent below what impartial observers believe minimally desirable'.

Cuts in services

These national figures mask wide differences between local authorities. Between 1979 and 1984:

● eight authorities had cut spending on Personal Social Services;

● 41 authorities – over one-third – had increased spending by less than 10 per cent (the minimum the government recognizes as necessary to maintain services);

● 84 authorities – over two-thirds – had increased spending by less than 20 per cent (the minimum the Directors of Social Services regard as necessary).

The emerging general picture is one of a decline in spending relative to demand in the largely Tory counties; while spending in the largely Labour metropolitan districts and Inner London boroughs has been increasing.

This pattern has exaggerated the already wide differences in the level of services provided by different authorities.

• In Labour-controlled Camden the number of home helps per 1,000 population over 65 rose from 13 in 1978-9 to an estimated 14 in 1984-5. In Tory Wiltshire, there were 6 home helps per 1,000 population over 65 in 1978-9, and an estimated 5.5 in 1984-5. DHSS guidelines in the late 1970s suggested 12.

The victims

Everyone has suffered from the squeeze on local authority expenditure. But the very elderly are perhaps the chief victims.

• In 1984 the House of Commons Social Services Committee revealed that 'figures of services for the elderly provided by the department show clearly that local-authority-supported residential care places are not keeping pace with the number of those over 75'; 'the number of meals served in people's homes or at day centres has not kept pace with the numbers of elderly people'.

• Holidays for the elderly and handicapped have been cut back heavily. Figures given to the committee show that between 1980 and 1983 expenditure fell by 12 per cent; the number of people helped declined by nearly 7 per cent.

The very young and people with disabilities were also early casualties of government-enforced cuts. In evidence to the House of Commons Social Services Committee in 1982, the Association of Directors of Social Services said:

In the first round of cuts in 1979-80 the budget for giving aids and adaptations for the physically handicapped was a natural target for almost every local authority that had to make cuts – thus causing great problems now, several years later.

We were particularly disturbed this year to see quite a considerable cut-back in the sort of services where we are helping families with very young children: cut-backs in social work services, fieldwork services, day-care services, day nurseries, quite a substantial cut-back in staffing in day nurseries.

Rate-capped

Labour local authorities – committed to good-quality services for those in need – have been forced to protect services by putting up rates. From April 1985, 18 local authorities, 14 of them social service authorities, will no longer have this option under the government's Rates Act 1984. Other local authorities will face increasingly severe penalties through the withdrawal of government grant if they continue to spend above the levels the government deems adequate. They will be forced to make major cuts in services.

● **Haringey**'s Director of Social Services forecasts that the 13.4 per cent cut the government desires would mean freezing all posts, no longer admitting children and old people to services and the closure of a number of homes and day centres.

● In **Southwark**, a cut of £5.5 million from the £30 million social services budget would mean the closure of several day centres for the elderly and handicapped and the loss of 80 jobs.

● In **Islington**, the social services share of £8.5 million cuts would mean the closure of two old people's homes, six day nurseries, day centres for the elderly and a reduction in home help and meals-on-wheels services.

Local authorities will have to start cutting their statutory services. They are being placed in an impossible dilemma: if they are to obey the government's Rates Act, they will have to default on other statutory obligations – under the Chronically Sick and Disabled Persons Act or Children and Young Persons Act, for instance.

Charges

Squeezed between government cuts in their Rate Support Grant and increased demand, some local authorities have introduced or massively increased charges for their services.

- In 1982–3, £327 million was raised through charges by English social services authorities, compared to £202 million in 1978–9.
- In 1982–3, charges were raised by 5 per cent or more in three-quarters of all authorities for meals-on-wheels; in nearly half the authorities for home helps; and in more than half the authorities for day-nursery places.

A new role for social services departments

The government's financial constraints on social services spending are part of a wider strategy to reduce the role of the public sector in meeting social needs. In a speech to the Directors of Social Services in Buxton (September 1984), Norman Fowler said that local authorities must make better use of the voluntary and private sectors. Social services departments should take on a more 'strategic enabling role', rather than trying to provide every necessary service themselves. The government is issuing a consultative document on this new role for social services departments.

The boom in private homes for old people

Privatization has already been gathering momentum under the Tories' strictures on spending. Private residential homes are booming, as local authority services fail to meet rising demand and the DHSS underwrites their fees. While the government has forced local authorities to close homes through a reduction in the Rate Support Grant, it has been giving public handouts to the private sector. Between 1978–9 and 1982–3:

- The number of people over 65 living in voluntary or private residential homes increased from under 36,000 to nearly 57,000. During the same period, the number of elderly people in local authority homes fell by 1,650.
- The number of elderly people having their fees paid by the DHSS more than doubled, from 11,000 to 23,000. The total amount paid by the DHSS increased ninefold, to £90 million.

In November 1983, Rhodes Boyson, then Social Security Minister, attempted to stop the spiralling cost of private residential care by fixing local maximum levels for charges. But the measure backfired as residential home owners put their fees up to the maximum and, by 1984, DHSS payments had rocketed to £200 million.

Standards of care are variable within the private sector, and where profit-making is the main motive, cutting costs has great attraction, leading to serious consequences for the care of elderly people. Nor is there any adequate system of accountability. While private homes have to be registered with local authorities, and local authorites have duties of inspection, the financial constraints faced by many local authorities limit their monitoring role.

In November 1984 the government proposed setting national maximum charges that can be met by the DHSS, to be effective from March 1985. But if local authorities are prevented from making adequate provision themselves, it will be elderly people who lose out. Many old people are in jeopardy.

Voluntary organizations

The government is also looking to voluntary organizations to fill the gap left by cuts in local authority spending. But the voluntary organizations themselves are feeling the pinch of government policies on local government.

The abolition of the GLC and metropolitan counties will cut off an important source of funding for voluntary organizations which will not be picked up by other local authorities. In 1983–4 the GLC gave £43 million to voluntary and community organizations and budgeted for £53 million in 1984–5. The National Council for Voluntary Organizations estimates that the metropolitan counties spend about £14 million a year in supporting voluntary and community organizations.

The government's proposals for funding voluntary organizations after the abolition of the GLC and metropolitan counties are totally inadequate and will lead to the demise of many schemes. The government's proposals, issued in September 1984, are:

● District councils would be given powers collectively to impose a levy on their authorities to raise up to £10 million in London and £3 million in the metropolitan counties, to support voluntary organizations which serve more than one district.

● Transitional arrangements would be made whereby the government would make available £3.7 million over four years to help authorities support voluntary organizations within their own boundaries. (These groups are currently financed by the GLC or metropolitan counties.) The district authority would have to meet 25 per cent of the grant.

These proposals leave a considerable shortfall on the money currently available to voluntary organizations. In London alone, the shortfall would be in the region of £30–40 million. And it is doubtful if the district authorities or London boroughs would even be able to participate in these limited proposals for fear of rate-capping or financial penalties.

Those voluntary organizations which depend upon funding from their local authority are also in danger from rate-capping and stiffer financial penalties. Whenever voluntary organizations have voiced their fears to ministers, they have been told to seek funds from industry, commerce or private individuals. But the voluntary organizations know how ungenerous such sources can be. Between 1975–6 and 1980–1 charities' net income from private funding and donations fell by 40 per cent in real terms.

Education

■ *We must restore to every child, regardless of background, the chance to progress as his or her abilities allow.*

Conservative manifesto, 1979

The Tories are constantly cutting education provision and opportunities across the whole of education from nursery education to adult education.

> ■ *I think I am presiding at the moment over an education system in which there really is inadequate provision for a very substantial minority.*
>
> Sir Keith Joseph, Secretary of State for Education,
> 20 February 1983

The level of spending on education has virtually stood still in real terms since 1978–9 at about £12.5 billion, despite – not because of – government policy. This is because Labour local authorities have spent in excess of government targets to protect services; many Tory authorities have cut provision. The net result is that actual education spending was 7.5 per cent above government plans for 1983–4.

Capping opportunities

The Tories' answer is to force local authorities to keep within targets by increasing penalties and, worse, by rate-capping. The government has decided to rate-cap four Labour LEAs – Brent, Haringey, ILEA and Sheffield. Haringey, with a possible cut of £9 million in 1985–6, could lose nearly 1,000 jobs in education, all of its 4,000 places in pre-school education, its school milk and meals services. It would have to cut books and equipment and to close almost all of its adult education and its youth services.

ILEA under attack

The government in its White Paper *Streamlining the Cities* proposed that London's education should no longer be administered by a single body, most of whose councillors are directly elected. Sir Keith Joseph wanted a board composed entirely of members nominated by the boroughs.

The response of Londoners to this proposal was hostile. The Local Government Bill abolishing the GLC will not abolish ILEA but will set up a new, directly elected ILEA in 1986. But the Bill gives powers to the Secretary of State to abolish it in the future. The new authority's performance will be reviewed by 1991, after which all its functions could be transferred to the Inner London boroughs. The Bill also gives the Education Secretary powers to control the staffing levels and management of the new ILEA for the first three years of its existence. Sir Keith Joseph has told ILEA that it is 'flabby' and can easily cut £57 million. But this would mean the loss of thousands of teaching and support jobs, and serious damage to the provision of books and equipment.

Under-fives under fire

> *If they [nurseries] are made available at public expense too readily, they can all too easily be seen as the expression of a philosophy which preaches that parents can do as they like and it is the duty of the state to look after children.*
>
> Patrick Jenkin MP, then Secretary of State for Social Services, speaking at the National Children's Bureau Conference, October 1979

Only 22 per cent of 3- and 4-year-olds went to nursery schools and classes in England in 1983. If one includes rising fives (those children who will be five during the school year) attending infant schools, 71 per cent of 4-year-olds and 30 per cent of 3-year-olds receive education. Yet it was Margaret Thatcher herself who, as Secretary of State for Education, made the pledge in the 1972 White Paper that nursery provision would be available for 90 per cent of 4-year-olds and 50 per cent of 3-year-olds by 1982.

● Almost 70,000 3- and 4-year-olds are denied pre-school education. The number of children in full-time places fell from 244,000 to 238,000 between 1980 and 1983.

● Despite a large increase in spare places in infant schools caused by falling rolls, the chance of a nursery place depends almost wholly on where you happen to live. In Labour Hounslow, 65 per cent of 3- and 4-year-olds receive nursery education; in Tory Gloucestershire, none do.

Standards slipping

In their 1983 report, Her Majesty's Inspectors of Schools indicated that damage has already been done by the cuts. They said:

- 'In some cases the circumstances in which education takes place and the availability of appropriate resources in the right quantity was found to be such as to make worth-while learning well-nigh "impossible".'
- The overall quality of work was not deemed 'satisfactory or better' in one-quarter of primary and secondary classes.
- 'In primary schools, a shortage of suitable books was recorded in almost one-fifth of all the lessons seen . . .'
- 'In three-quarters of all schools visited, parental contributions were said to be moderate or substantial.' In some schools in Kent, bingo sessions are being held to raise funds for essential equipment.

The Tory answer to these reports is to shoot the messenger. The Chair of the Conservative National Advisory Committee on Education, with the approval of Bob Dunn, the Junior Minister, is urging Tory leaders of LEAs to call for the banning of the annual HMI reports.

Class sizes

In spite of falling rolls, as many as 1.4 million children are in classes of over 30; 130,000 are in classes of over 35. Although the national pupil–teacher ratio has not worsened, there has been deterioration in many LEAs.

- 57 LEAs (60 per cent) had not improved their pupil–teacher ratios in one or more sectors – nursery, primary and secondary – between 1979 and 1983. Yet school rolls had fallen dramatically over that period.
- There is a wide variation between LEAs in pupil–teacher ratios, with Labour ILEA having the best ratio of 13.8:1 and Tory Somerset having the worst of 20.6:1.
- The number of teachers has been cut – from 438,000 in 1979–80 to 408,000 in 1983–4; it is planned to drop to between 386,000 and 390,000 in 1986–7. Yet the government's Advisory Committee on the Supply and Education of Teachers says that 46,000 more teachers will be needed by 1993.
- There is a particular shortage in teachers in some subjects.

The 1983 HMI report revealed: 'In one school, only one of the five full-time teachers of mathematics had a qualification in the subject.'

Teachers' pay
● Teachers' pay has fallen by nearly one-third in real terms, since the Houghton Report on teachers' pay ten years ago.
● Thousands of teachers are on relatively low pay because falling rolls have reduced the number of promotions available.

But when Keith Joseph was asked why an 18-year-old trainee police officer was paid more than many school teachers, he stated it was simply an illustration of the law of supply and demand. Teachers were forced to take industrial action in 1984 over the derisory pay offer of 3 per cent. Only after a lengthy and bitter dispute did the Secretary of State agree on arbitration which awarded teachers a slightly improved increase of 5 per cent.

The government now wants to impose a 'payment by results' system whereby teachers assessed as 'very good' would be given more money than others; those deemed 'unsatisfactory' would be dismissed.

Comprehensives in the firing line
Ninety per cent of local authority pupils attend comprehensive schools, but fully comprehensive education is a long way off. The Tories' Education Act 1979 allows Tory local authorities to keep the unfair 11-plus.

In 1983, Bob Dunn, Junior Minister for Schools, told the Conservative Education Committee, that parents must have the 'freedom to have grammar schools' – and, of course, imposing secondary-modern-type schools on the majority of pupils. This was a green light to Tory councils to turn the clock back and scrap their comprehensives. But opposition from parents and teachers in areas such as Richmond and Solihull has so far thwarted Tory plans.

Private schools: the public Bill
Private schools harm the state sector by poaching the

brightest pupils from comprehensive schools. The Tories' Assisted Places Schemes used taxpayers' money to buy places for over 13,000 pupils in private schools in 1983–4. The private school Bill which the taxpayers pay is as follows:

- Assisted Places Scheme: £15 million;
- Local authority place-buying (excluding special education): £25 million;
- Ministry of Defence place-buying: £57 million;
- Foreign Office place-buying: £6 million;
- tax and rate relief: £26 million.

No hope for the handicapped
The Warnock Report on special education proposed the integration of most pupils with special needs (as a result of physical or mental handicaps) within ordinary schools. But the government has refused to provide any extra cash to implement the proposals contained in its Education Act 1981. According to the National Union of Teachers, one in ten local education authorities is breaking the law by failing to provide full-time study for handicapped pupils up to the age of 19.

Food for thought
The Tories' Education Act 1980 encouraged LEAs to dismantle their school meals service and end school milk by removing their duties to make such provision. The government is planning a cut in these services of as much as 38 per cent in 1984–5. Some Tory authorities, such as Merton, have abolished all school meals and meet their minimum legal duty to provide meals for poor and handicapped pupils by giving them just a few sandwiches.

Given a caning
In February 1982 the European Court of Human Rights ruled that the government's policy of allowing schools to administer corporal punishment to all children, regardless of the views of parents, was in breach of the European Convention on Human Rights. Instead of banning corporal punishment in all schools, the government is introducing a

Bill which will allow pupils whose parents oppose corporal punishment to opt out of it. Schools would have to compile 'hit lists' of those pupils who could be caned. Even the Tory-controlled Association of County Councils has said: 'a system which allowed different sanctions for the same misdemeanour . . . would be difficult to justify and might be regarded by some as lacking morality.'

Parent power

The government fantasizes that standards can be raised by giving parents control of governing bodies. In his Green Paper *Parental Influence at School* (1984), Sir Keith Joseph rejects the proposals in Labour's Taylor Report for an equal partnership between local authorities, teachers and parents in the running of schools. Instead, he wants the majority of governors to be elected parents. Local authority associations, teachers' unions and even parents' organizations see the proposal as impracticable.

What is taught

Sir Keith Joseph wishes to introduce a nationally agreed curriculum which cuts out 'clutter'. But for 'clutter' read what Tories disapprove of – peace studies and political education, sociology, sex education, etc.

He has, however, moved to introduce a common system of examination at 16-plus by merging O-levels and CSEs. But his method of doing it – introducing special 'distinction' and 'merit' certificates for the top-ability range – will preserve the O-level in all but name.

Further and higher education

The government is cutting opportunities at a time when the number of young people is at its peak.

In the universities:
● Income has been cut by 9 per cent between 1980–1 and 1983–4.
● The cuts have been administered unfairly by the University Grants Committee (UGC), some universities have had to cut their income by 1 per cent; others, like Salford, have had

to make a cut of 28 per cent, and Bradford a cut of 19 per cent.

● As many as 15,000 people with A-level grades sufficient to gain entry to university a few years ago were refused a place in 1984–5.

● One in six teaching posts has been axed since 1979 through early retirement – at the cost of £80 million of taxpayers' money.

Since 1979, the UGC has acted as the government's poodle, meekly obeying its commands: now fed up with being kicked around, it has finally turned on its master. Its 1984 Strategy Document stated:

> These cuts were so severe that great harm has been done. Academic planning has been disrupted, morale has been impaired, thousands of young people have been denied university education, confidence in government has been shaken and will be difficult to restore.

In further education
(See training section.)

In the polytechnics:
● Due to the cuts in university places there has been a very rapid rise in the number of students – an extra 53,000 – with a significant drop in the level of spending per student, a cut of one-fifth.

● Worse is to come. Those polytechnics that have received 'topping up' from their LEAs face the prospect of losing it as penalties and rate-capping further restrict local authority spending.

The government's National Advisory Body (NAB) responsible for higher education has admitted that it is 'not possible to achieve the triple objectives of access, maintenance of standards, and a continued downward move of the unit of resource [cost per student]' (NAB Report 1984).

Adult education

- The government is planning a cut of 30 per cent in adult education spending for 1984–5.
- Adult education fees are shooting up as a direct result of government policy – not surprising when the minister responsible, Peter Brooke, has stated that 'adult education is undervalued because it is underpriced'.
- Grants to university extra-mural departments are being cut by as much as 14 per cent, which will mean sharp increases in fees; the Workers' Education Assocation grant is being cut by 8 per cent over a three-year period from 1983–4.
- The Open University's grant has fallen by 4 per cent in real terms since 1980. Fees for each credit course have doubled since 1980 to £133 – making the cost prohibitive to the very people for whom the university was set up. The government is planning deeper cuts and the university has had to make cuts of £3.5 million in 1984; £10 million by 1986.
- Sir Keith Joseph is even trying to undermine academic freedom. He has accused the Open University of left-wing Marxist bias and asked it to change its economics course.

Student grants: pay as you learn

The government's proposals to increase the amount parents pay for their children's higher education has touched a very raw middle-class nerve. Tory MPs' postbags were full of letters from irate parents. Thousands of students marched on parliament. Over 100 Tory backbenchers signed highly critical motions. Sir Keith Joseph's package included:

- A 3 per cent increase in the level of grants, even though their value has fallen by 14 per cent since 1979.
- Major changes to the scale of parental contributions. All parents with residual incomes of more than £13,000 per annum would be expected to pay more towards the maintenance of their children at college.
- The abolition of the minimum grant of £205 – following its halving from £410 in 1983–4 – withdrawing a safety-net for many students.
- Charging parents part of the costs of education, with some

parents paying £520 a year towards tuition fees.

The deal affected 183,000 students. A total of 53,000 parents were asked to make a contribution towards tuition fees. These changes would cut student incomes further. The government is using the grants system to reduce demand and cut places in higher education.

In the face of a Tory rebellion, Sir Keith made a humiliating climbdown. Or at least that's how it appeared. Charging parents part of the fees has been dropped. But the other measures stand. And in announcing his U-turn, he revealed another nasty surprise – the possibility of introducing student loans.

To pay for the U-turn the government has to find £21 million. It could easily find this sum by abolishing the Assisted Places Scheme which pours £21 million of tax-payers' money a year into the coffers of private schools. But instead, the Tories are to lop £11 million off state education – from university equipment, science research and adult education. The other £10 million will be 'found' by the Chancellor.

Thatcher has been forced to turn. Can we now expect Tory backbenchers to rebel over worse injustices? Like the cut in living standards of the old, the disabled, the jobless? Like the destruction of the welfare state? Like the plight of the homeless?

Training

Training is essential if we are to update the skills of our workforce and improve our industrial performance.

Britain lags far behind other industrial countries in the provision of training. Just a third of our workforce has any recognized qualification equivalent to at least one O-level. That compares with about two-thirds in West Germany and Japan and over three-quarters in the United States.

● Young people leaving our schools today have little prospect of quality training compared with many countries in the EEC. In France, 40 per cent of the 16–18 age group are on full-time vocational training courses compared with only 19 per cent in Britain.

● For adults, the position is even worse. In West Germany 40 adults undergo training for every one in Britain.

The Tories' record on training is appalling.

● **Apprenticeships providing craft training have been slashed.** The number of young people entering apprenticeship has been cut by half since 1979. The intake of engineering apprenticeships in 1984 reached an all-time low of 7,800.

● **Industrial training boards have been attacked.** Sixteen of the 23 boards have been scrapped. In the absence of any mechanism for sharing the costs of training, firms may once again 'poach' skilled labour rather than take on their own apprentices.

● **Skill centres are to be closed.** The government wants to close 29 skill centres which train young people on the Youth Training Scheme (YTS) and retrain adults. Over 1,000 training jobs will be axed.

● **YTS is being constantly undermined.** Despite the government's claims to have lavished expenditure on the scheme, it has simply plundered funds from other programmes such as adult training and made up the rest from the European Social Fund.

The government sees YTS not as a bridge between school and work, but as a way of fiddling the unemployment figures and cutting youth wages (see pages 145–9).

The quality of training on YTS is very variable. A recent report from Her Majesty's Inspectorate pinpointed widespread weaknesses in teaching, the structure and content of courses, staff development and equipment. In its 1984 review of YTS, the Manpower Services Commission (MSC) admitted that the scheme 'cannot guarantee . . . jobs'.

The government's treatment of trainees has forced many

young people to vote with their feet: only 350,000 of the 460,000 places were taken up by eligible 16- and 17-year-olds in 1984.

● **Opportunities for adults have been cut.** The Training Opportunities Programme has been cut. This has been especially harmful to the prospects of many women who would like to re-enter the labour market. Only 80,000 unemployed adults will be able to take part in training schemes this year.

The only substantial MSC scheme for the long-term unemployed adult is the Community Programme. It offers work of 'social value' on an hourly rate for the job – but no training at all.

The government has introduced a loans system for adult training. This would force individuals to pay for their own training – and allow employers to reap the benefit at no cost to themselves. It would result in a further contraction of adult training.

● **Training funds are being robbed from local authorities.** The government in its 1984 White Paper *Training for Jobs* decided to take a quarter of work-related further education from elected local education authorities. The LEAs are insisting, however, that they have a say in how it is to be spent.

In addition, technical education in schools is being directed by central government. In 1983 Thatcher announced, without prior consultation with LEAs, the Technical and Vocational Education Initiative. Under this scheme, the MSC fund pilot technical courses for 14–18-year-olds in school and colleges. Many educationalists are alarmed that this will establish a technical stream in comprehensive schools and reintroduce the old technical schools through the back door.

A few hard-pressed local authorities have joined the pilot schemes, attracted primarily by £25 million of new money over the five years from 1984. This would be channelled into a few selected schools. In most schools, however, the government's cuts are reducing the number of technical teachers and courses are being dropped. The scheme is now to be extended to 59 out of 104 LEAs in England and Wales and the government wants it eventually to cover all authorities.

Housing

■ *Our goal is to make Britain the best-housed nation in Europe.*
Tory manifesto, 1983

Since 1979 housing has borne the brunt of all public spending cuts. Housing expenditure has been cut by a massive 57 per cent.

● For every £100 spent on public housing in 1974–5, £21 will be spent in 1984–5 (after allowing for inflation).
● In 1974–5 nearly 10 per cent of total public expenditure was spent on housing. In 1984–5 it will be less than 3 per cent.
● The UK now spends by far the lowest proportion of its national income on housing of any country in the Common Market. All the other EEC countries spend between two and three times as much as Britain.

Successive governments since the Second World War made progress in clearing slums and improving housing conditions. Under the Tories that progress has come to a full stop. In fact, things are now getting worse, not better.

● Annual **slum clearance** has dwindled from 72,000 properties in 1971 to 20,000 in 1984.
● 30 per cent of today's **housing stock** was built before 1919.
● The Association of Metropolitan Authorities estimates that there is a shortage of 517,000 dwellings.

At current rates of house-building it would take to the year 2950 to replace the housing stock. What housing there is is often in a shocking state.

● 1.25 million dwellings in England and Wales are unfit for human habitation.

- 1 million dwellings in England and Wales lack one or more basic amenities.
- 2.5 million homes in the UK are seriously affected by damp.
- 3 million homes require repairs costing £2,300 or more.
- 1.5 million homes have serious design defects.

The housing crisis is not just about council housing. Council housing has particular problems and has faced disproportionate cuts. But the Tories laissez-faire housing policies have also hurt private tenants and low-income house-owners.

The Tories are increasing inequality in housing. General subsidies to council housing have been completely withdrawn from the majority of local authorities. In stark contrast, tax relief for owner-occupiers has continued to grow in real terms – and the richer you are, the more you get:

- council housing subsidy **decreased** from its 1975–6 level of £915 million to £393 million in 1984–5
- tax relief on mortgages **went up** from £1,100 million in 1975–6 to £3,500 million in 1984–5

The collapse of house-building
In 1981 house-building (public and private) fell to its lowest level since the 1920s. Since then, public sector house-building has remained almost unchanged, while private house-building has shown only a modest recovery and is now falling.

Public house-building has been slashed. Less than 40,000 new council houses were started in 1984: about 65 per cent down on 1978 and nearly 80 per cent down on 1975. The Tories say that the private sector can make up for this fall – but the construction industry is the first to agree that it can't.

Taking public and private house building *together*, homes started under the Tories are 40 per cent below the number started under Labour.

The building industry – hit both by the recession and cuts in public sector investment – is sharply critical of Tory policies. The President of the Building Employers' Confederation (BEC) described government policies as 'a kick in the teeth for construction'. In an interview in the *National Builder* (June 1984), he said:

> Since Mrs Thatcher first gained office in 1979 we have increasingly been subjected to an extreme form of disruptive and damaging 'stop–go' cycles; we have seen truly massive cuts in our capital construction programmes, a serious reduction in housing opportunities and appalling unemployment.

Latest government moves seem designed to make matters worse.

● In March 1984 the Tories extended VAT to house improvements.
● In July 1984 they announced a 'voluntary' moratorium on new council capital spending using 'brought forward' capital receipts. The BEC estimates that up to £2 billion-worth of local authority could be lost.
● In December 1984 capital programmes were cut by another £1 billion. Councils had been allowed to spend £40 per cent of the proceeds from council house sales on new housing investment – now they can only spend 20 per cent. Meanwhile the £1 billion stays in local authority bank accounts – they just can't spend it on housing!
● In addition, Ian Gow announced a further £65 million cut in housing expenditure – as if somehow it was a victory against Treasury demands for more. The Public Expenditure White Paper published in January 1985 makes it clear that the *real* cut – compared to the planned programme from the previous year – is £650 million.
● The government justification for further cuts is an accounting 'overspend' – although no individual council has overspent. Tory Sir Ian Gilmour called this the 'ridiculous results of Treasury dogmatism' (*Hansard*, 18 July 1984).
● The January 1985 White Paper also spells out the Government's intention to cut improvement grants, by introducing means testing and reducing the amount of repair work eligible for grant.

Putting the squeeze on private tenants

The private rented sector has been declining throughout the present century. By 1981 it accounted for 12.5 per cent of all dwellings. Private tenants often live in the worst housing and yet get little or no government help.

- A disproportionate number of private tenants are ethnic minority households.
- 17 per cent of privately tenanted homes are unfit.
- 13 per cent lack basic amenities.
- 300,000 households live in houses in multiple occupation; 77 per cent in sub-standard accommodation.
- Average rents of registered unfurnished tenancies have risen from £433 per annum in 1978 to £767 per annum in the second half of 1983.

Far from dealing with the problems, the Tories have taken a number of steps to strengthen the hand of private landlords over tenants. They have:

- allowed rents to be raised every two years, instead of three years as previously, where 'fair rents' are registered;
- shortened the phasing-in periods of increases in registered rents;
- applied 'fair rents' to some 200,000 properties in England and Wales lacking basic amenities and which had previously been subject to very low, controlled rents;
- introduced new types of tenure, without security for tenants and without controlled rent levels, for new tenancies granted after 1980.

More is to come. In October 1984 Norman Tebbit suggested that the Rents Acts should be further dismantled to 'revive' the private sector.

No help for home-owners

Despite their slogans about a 'property-owning democracy', the Tories have done little or nothing to help average home-owners. Many home-owners on low incomes, especially the elderly or unemployed, find it impossible to maintain or repair their homes.

● Disrepair is increasing fastest among owner-occupiers – one-fifth of privately owned homes are in need of repairs costing £2,500 or over.
● Nearly half the one million unfit properties are owner-occupied.
● The Tory abolition of minimum housing standards has encouraged the building of shoddy, cramped houses for first-time buyers.

House prices have risen sharply, leaving millions of people unable to buy their own home. Better-off home-owners get substantial government subsidy in the form of tax relief on mortgages. But low-income home-owners get little or no assistance. Under Labour, the mortgage rate was on average 10.75 per cent. Under the Tories it reached an all-time high of 15 per cent.

The collapse of the Building Societies' cartel means that many Building Societies are charging considerably more than the approved rate.

The attack on council tenants

Rents have been forced up for all council tenants. Each year the government has issued guidelines for rent increases to be applied by local authorities. Though not binding, these guidelines have been reinforced by cuts in central government housing subsidies and by cuts in Rate Support Grant which have affected all council services.

The average weekly local authority rent in England and Wales has gone up from £6.40 in April 1979 under Labour to £14.70 in April 1984: a real increase of 40 per cent. Over 3.5 million tenants cannot afford to pay the high rents, and receive housing benefit help. But since 1983 housing benefits have been cut as well (see pages 130–31).

Central government housing subsidies in England (excluding housing benefit) have been cut from an average of £448 per dwelling in 1979–80 to an estimated £93 in 1984–5 (in 1982–3 prices). Subsidies met from local rates have also been reduced. In fact, rents now subsidize rates in many local authority areas.

Council tenants face growing repair problems – as public expenditure cuts make it increasingly difficult for cash-starved councils to repair and maintain their homes. But instead of tackling these problems, the Tories introduced what they call a 'right to repair'. Tenants will be able to get repairs done by private contractors – and charge the council. However, tenants' organizations fear that these proposals will reduce tenant protection – by making tenants responsible for the quality of work, and leaving them vulnerable to fly-by-night operators. The scheme is inadequate, bureaucratic, and could backfire on tenants. It falls far short of Labour's proposals and of the repair rights already enjoyed by tenants in several Labour authorities. More serious still are the problems of defects in system-built housing.

● The Association of Metropolitan Authorities estimates that £5,000 million will be needed to remedy design and construction defects in tower blocks and other high-density estates build in the 1960s and 1970s.
● A further £5,000 million will be required to tackle defects in local authority housing built earlier in the postwar period.

And these estimates do not include finance to deal with heating, insulation, noise or environment problems which make a much larger number of high-rise blocks and large estates unacceptable homes for the 1980s.

The government's only response has been the inadequate and inequitable Housing Defects Act under which:

● Only 29 'systems' have been identified as eligible for assistance – even though some 300 non-traditional building systems have been used. The government is clearly more interested in defective houses with gardens – which are more likely to have been bought – than defective blocks of flats. For example, neither Bison nor the notorious Ronan Point flats have been included.

● People who have *bought* these defective council homes will be able to get a 90 per cent grant to repair them – or will be entitled to sell them back to the local authority. But local authorities, who own 90 per cent of these defective dwellings, will get no extra help to deal with the problems *either* of the housing they already own *or* of those they are forced to buy back.

● Councils like Newham, forced to demolish blocks such as Ronan Point because they are unsafe, will get no extra help. Many more local authorities would like to demolish hard-to-let flats and build houses with gardens. But the Tories won't let them.

The Tories' solution to poor-quality council housing is simple – sell it. To companies or speculators – or tenants. In the words of Margaret Thatcher:

> Mothers with small children living in tower blocks will, under a Conservative government, now have three options. To carry on renting, to put down an option to purchase the flat within a reasonable time, or to purchase the flat. That seems to me to enlarge the freedom and possibilities available to such people.

The Tories want to see council housing become residual 'welfare housing' for the very poorest households – when everyone who can afford to has been bribed, cajoled or forced to buy. At the same time as cutting back on council building and pushing up rents, they have forced councils to sell off housing to sitting tenants wishing to buy.

Only the best council housing can be sold – the more attractive houses with gardens, rather than properties on the less desirable estates. So councils are left with the least desirable properties to house the homeless, applicants from the waiting lists, and tenants needing transfers to more suitable accommodation. The housing prospects for those who cannot afford to buy become more and more depressing.

Under the 'right to buy' legislation, substantial discounts on the market price must be offered to long-standing tenants.

By March 1984, 600,000 council properties had been sold to tenants in Great Britain. These discounts, worth over £3,000 million, are enough to pay for:

- 100,000 new homes; or
- 500,000 improvement grants for existing private sector housing.

The Housing Building and Control Act 1984 extends the right to buy even further – increasing discounts and forcing councils to sell off even badly needed homes adapted for the disabled.

The government has launched a £1.4 million publicity campaign to promote the 'right to buy'. That sum alone could build 50 new homes. But the main point is that there are *too few* council homes available to meet the current, and growing, demand for homes to *rent*:

- There are now 1,200,000 households registered on local authority housing waiting lists in England.
- There are 500,000 overcrowded or concealed households.
- There were 78,000 households accepted as homeless in 1983 compared to 57,000 in 1979. Many more homeless people, especially single people, go uncounted.

Transport

Public transport services have been hit hard by the Tory government. And worse is yet to come. In pursuit of their obsession with 'market forces', the Tories are preventing the development of a sensible, integrated transport network run in the interests of the public. Instead, the prospect is for more cuts in a vicious circle of declining services and higher fares.

Local transport under attack
Cuts in government spending, restrictions on local government and damaging Tory legislation have all led to cuts in bus services in many parts of the country:

- Transport Supplementary Grant (TSG) – paid by central government to local government for transport purposes – is being cut. In 1984–5 it was already 23 per cent lower than when the Tories took office. Now the government is removing TSG competely for public transport expenditure, keeping it only for certain road building.
- New Bus Grant, which was paid towards the cost of buying new buses has now been phased out completely.
- Bus fares have increased, on average, by 82 per cent since 1979 – 11 per cent in real terms.

The Transport Act 1980 swept away many long-standing licensing provisions and was designed to make it easier for private operators to compete with public services. But by creaming off the traffic on the most profitable routes, private operators have made it harder for public operators to maintain 'unprofitable', but socially necessary, services.

The Tories now intend to go further with new legislation which threatens to destroy what remains of the bus network. Their 1985 Transport Bill – based on their 1984 Buses White Paper – would lead to a virtual free-for-all, by:

- scrapping the present route-licensing system completely;
- preventing cross-subsidies which help maintain networks;
- breaking up of the National Bus Company, municipal bus undertakings, and the public transport networks in the metropolitan counties.

In the words of the non-political *Buses* magazine (September 1984), the White Paper represents 'the mindless pursuit of political dogma with very little thought for the consequences'.

The government has been warned by almost everyone involved in the bus industry of the damage it will do. For instance, on 10 October 1984 the transport conference of the Tory-controlled Association of District Councils concluded – unanimously – that:

> most of the proposals . . . are both untried and impracticable and will seriously threaten the quality and

efficiency of local bus services in town and country to the detriment of the travelling public.

Many more people will be condemned to virtual isolation as a result of the Tory government's policies. Already, many parts of the country have seen cut-backs.

● The National Bus Company's operating mileage fell by 15 per cent between 1979 and 1983.
● Many places have few or no services in the evening or on Sundays.
● Some communities have found themselves completely cut off from the transport network.

Under the Tories, this trend is set to continue.

In the Labour-controlled conurbations, the story so far has been different. Labour councils have followed policies to support public transport and hold or reduce fares wherever possible.

● South Yorkshire's cheap fares policy has shown, over a number of years, how the decline in public transport can be halted.
● In London, the GLC's 'Fares Fair' policy was ruled illegal following court action brought by a Tory council. The government refused to intervene, and fares doubled as a result. However, a second attempt in London – when fares were reduced by 25 per cent in 1983 and steps taken towards achieving further integration – has proved successful, with a big increase in public transport usage and a reduction in traffic congestion.

But the Tories couldn't stomach Labour councils looking after the users of public transport.

● The Transport Act 1983 tried to limit subsidies to public transport from the metropolitan counties and the GLC by providing for government-imposed 'guidelines' and inviting legal challenge to any spending above those levels.

● The London Regional Transport Act 1984 removed control of London Transport from the GLC, placing it in the hands of an unelected quango. The government, which controls the purse-strings, is encouraging moves towards disintegration and private competition. It is cutting the level of subsidy by half. Fares rose in January 1985. And 6,000 job losses are planned over the next three years. At the same time, when taking over London Transport, the Transport Secretary, according to a High Court ruling, took £50 million more from the GLC – and thus London ratepayers – than he was entitled to.

● The government's plans to abolish the GLC and the metropolitan counties will, if they go through, fragment responsibility for transport policies and planning and stop much-needed co-ordination. Worse services, higher fares and chaos on the roads will inevitably result.

Railways in danger

Britain's rail network is also suffering as a result of Tory policies. The government says there should be no major route closures. But its policies are making a decline in the level and quality of services almost inevitable.

The 1983 Serpell Report was commissioned by a government concerned more with financial objectives than the needs of the travelling public. The report included proposals for higher fares, poorer services, fewer jobs, reduced maintenance, and possibly even lower safety standards. There were also 'options' which would leave vast areas of the country without a railway. The Tories' response has been ambiguous and there is still the threat of a 'Serpell by stealth' policy. Already under this government:

● Investment has been cut back sharply. In 1983, investment was £160 million less in real terms than in 1979.
● Fares on British Rail have increased by more than 80 per cent since 1979 – 8 per cent in real terms.
● British Rail has shed 39,000 jobs between 1980 and 1983.

Financial support for British Rail is lower than for railways in most continental countries. Latest available figures show that the rate of support for British Rail is less than half that for eight other European countries. However, Transport Secretary Nicholas Ridley has said that the level of government grant – £837 million in 1984 – must be cut by £200 million by 1986. Services must therefore continue to deteriorate.

- Current plans will mean the closure of 1,900 miles of track and a reduction of a further 25,000 jobs.
- BR's 1984 timetable brought in significant service cuts, notably in London and the south-east. Some actual line closures are still in the pipeline, including the first main line closure for many years, between Settle and Carlisle. London's Marylebone Station is also threatened.
- Changes in Transport Supplementary Grant and the plans to abolish the metropolitan counties represent a further threat to local rail services.

Heavier Lorries

At the same time as encouraging the run-down of public transport, the government has allowed bigger and heavier lorries on to Britain's roads. It has:

- increased the maximum weight for lorries from 32.5 tonnes to 38 tonnes;
- increased the maximum speed limit on dual carriageways for heavy lorries from 40mph to 50mph;
- threatened to block plans by the GLC for a night-time and weekend ban on most heavy lorries.

The heaviest lorries cause the greatest damage. There is already a massive backlog of costly work which needs to be done to strengthen bridges to cope with heavy vehicles. The restrictions on the Severn Bridge and the closure of Hammersmith Bridge across the Thames illustrate the problem. In both cases, the damage has been attributed to the impact of heavy lorries.

Privatized transport

The Tories' passion for 'privatization' has been particularly evident in transport.

● The National Freight Corporation, British Transport Docks Board and various British Rail subsidiaries have already been sold off.
● Still threatened with privatization are British Airways, National Bus Company and other parts of the public transport network.

Public enterprises have been sold off at knockdown prices with no regard for the interests of users – or taxpayers. Another example of private profit taking priority over public need in Thatcher's Britain.

The Alliance in local government

The Liberals have a total of 2,127 seats in local government and control six councils: Chelmsford, Hereford, North-east Fife and Medina (Isle of Wight) District Councils; the London Borough of Richmond; and the Isle of Wight. The SDP has a mere 313 seats, and controls no councils. Nor does it hold the balance of power anywhere.

The Liberals' record in local government leaves a lot to be desired – reflecting their support for many of the policies of Thatcher. On numerous occasions they sided with the Tories against Labour *before* the May 1984 local government elections:

● In **Bradford** (Tory–Liberal control) the Liberals voted with the Tories to reintroduce home help charges.
● In **Bristol** (Tory–Liberal control) the Liberals backed a Tory asset-stripping plan involving council land and buildings worth over £50 million.
● In **Cambridge** (minority Labour administration) the Liberals voted against Labour's £0.25 million Job Creation Programme.

- In **Lothian**, Scotland (Tory–Alliance control) the Alliance group voted to end concessionary free travel for the elderly – introduced by the previous Labour administration.
- In **Pendle** (minority Labour administration) the Liberals and the Tories blocked vitally important Urban Aid Schemes when they came up for renewal.
- In **Walsall** (Tory–Liberal control) the Liberals voted with the Tories to withdraw free buses for blind people under retirement age.

Since May 1984:

- In **Hammersmith** (Tory–Liberal control) the Liberals and the Tories closed a children's home following a £155,000 **cut** in the children's home budget for 1984–5. A *cut* of £800,000 in the social services budget is planned for 1985–6.
- In **Waltham Forest** (Tory–Liberal control) the Liberals supported a Tory proposal to sell off council-owned land. The effect is that new-build council housing is coming to an end. Renovated council housing has also been sold; an open-air swimming pool closed and demolished; and several secondary schools closed, and the buildings and land are to be sold off.

For most of the time between 1973 and 1983 the Liberals controlled Liverpool council with Tory support. It is well to remind ourselves of their record over the last four years of this period, from 1979 to 1983:

- the cost of **school meals** was increased – up from 25p to 55p;
- a **social services meal** cost you twice as much – up from 24p to 48p;
- **day nursery** charges were doubled – up from £1.80 to £3.60 per week;
- **burial costs** were more than doubled – up from £44 to £91;
- **council rents** for a typical two-bedroomed flat were increased – up an average of £10 per week.

2. Britain broke

Britain's economy has been devastated by Thatcher's Tories. Unemployment has reached record levels. Whole industries have been laid to waste. The nation's essential assets have been sold off to speculators. The North Sea oil windfall has been squandered in payment for the government's reckless excursion into monetarism. Britain has been turned into a low-wage, no-tech, 'shoeshine' economy; an economy that won't be able to pay its way when the oil runs out.

Instead of strengthening British industry so that it can meet the challenge of the twenty-first century, the Tories have plunged the economy back into the nineteenth century. The costs of their folly have been enormous; costs that cannot be simply accounted for in pounds, shillings and pence; costs that include untold human suffering, untold misery and hardship. In taking Britain back into the past, they have wiped out the future for millions of people. They stand accused of wilful, criminal neglect. The British people are bound to find them guilty.

What crisis? This crisis

■ *Crisis is the anxiety of parents, the hopelessness of children, the graduates taking temporary clerking jobs, the families being split and scattered as they search for work around the country – and all because of the level of unemployment.*
Neil Kinnock, *Hansard*, 30 October 1984

■ *Crisis? What crisis? There is no crisis.*
Nigel Lawson, *Times*, 19 August 1984

Despite Tory Chancellor Nigel Lawson's claim that there is

no crisis, there *is* a crisis facing Britain. A *growing* crisis of:

● **Record unemployment.** In January 1985, 3,341,000 people were 'officially' unemployed.
● **Record bankruptcies.** There were 8,217 bankruptcies in England and Wales in 1984, 17 per cent more than in 1983.
● **Record imports.** Britain now buys more manufactured goods from abroad than it sells overseas, for the first time *ever*.

And it's going to get worse. We are being left without the technologies and skills to produce the goods and services of the future:

● Nearly £50,000 million of private investment went overseas between 1979 and 1983.
● Investment in British manufacturing is down by a quarter on its 1979 level. This compares with a slight increase over the previous five years.

So much for Margaret Thatcher's claim that 'basically, the economy is still in good shape' (*Guardian*, 13 July 1984).

Britain isn't working
■ *There is every prospect that by next year we will see the start of a fall in the level of unemployment.*
> Nigel Lawson, *Guardian*, 21 May 1983

Nigel Lawson, faced with record unemployment figures and reminded of the above forecast, commented (*Times*, 28 September 1984), 'The year's not out, but it may well be proved wrong.'

Over 3,300,000 people are registered as unemployed. Each month, new record levels of unemployment are being announced. And this ignores the 'forgotten unemployed' (see page 80). So much for Tory claims of a recovery which was going to cut unemployment.

'The revival is started and I want it to gather pace,' promised Margaret Thatcher in an ITN (5 January 1984) interview at the start of 1984. But by 11 October the same year, the *Engineer* was not so sure: 'The much vaunted recovery is spluttering, and some sectors of industry are still waiting for the upturn.'

The forgotten unemployed. The official UK unemployment figure – 3.3 million – counts only those claiming benefits. The real job shortage is at least 4 million, when we include those on government schemes and those (mainly married women) who would like a job but do not claim benefits.

Long-term unemployed. Over 1.3 million people have been out of work for more than a year and they now account for 40 per cent of the unemployed. The number who have been unemployed for two years has increased by a third between 1983 and 1984.

Unemployment in the regions. January 1985: Northern Ireland is the worst hit with 21 per cent unemployed, followed by the North (19 per cent), Wales (17 per cent) and the North-west (17 per cent.)

Young people. Over 1.2 million are unemployed – 39 per cent of the total – 353,000 of them for over a year.

Women. Over 1 million are officially unemployed, but this understates the true figure because so many women do not register. Women's unemployment has more than tripled since May 1979, compared with an increase of around 2.5 times for men.

Higher death-rate for unemployed. Unemployment may be responsible for the deaths of 280,000 this year, according to a government study, *Unemployment, Health and Social Policy*. It found that death-rates among the unemployed seeking work was 20 per cent higher than expected. One in four young people who are unemployed has contemplated suicide, reported the study *Young and Unemployed*.

The number of hours lost through short-time working doubled between April and August 1984, to 1 million. And the number of jobs being created has fallen dramatically:

● Only 10,000 jobs were created in all industries and services in April, May and June 1984 – half as many as in the same period of 1983, and nine times less than in the final three months of 1983.
● In the service sector – where the Tories say the jobs are going to come from – only 36,000 jobs were created in April, May and June 1984, compared with 85,000 in the same three months of 1983.
● Moreover, the vast majority of the jobs that have been created have been *part-time* jobs. These have been filled by women, at the same time as the number of full-time jobs has fallen.

Official unemployment will reach 4 million by 1990, predict two influential forecasters – the Cambridge Econometrics Group and the Institute of Employment, Warwick University (*Guardian*, 9 January 1984; *Observer*, 31 July 1983). While City brokers Grieveson Grant predict that the *real* level of unemployment will be 4.8 million by 1987 (*Daily Mirror*, 24 October 1984).

Lawson's illusion
■ *We will see the recovery spread more widely throughout the economy . . . Critics who said there could be no recovery without the government's stimulus have been proved wrong. Those who now argue that the recovery was not sustainable, that it was unbalanced and that inflation was bound to rise again were wrong.*

Nigel Lawson, *Times*, 29 September 1983

More jobs are needed, but there's little prospect that they will be created. Britain's economy is still far weaker than when Labour left office, despite the Tory 'upturn'. In the third quarter of 1984:

● National was only 2 per cent above its 1979 level, and non-oil output was the same as in 1979.

- Industrial output was 6 per cent below its 1979 level.
- Manufacturing output was a massive 9 per cent below its 1979 level.

The growth slowdown is not due to the miners' strike, say stockbrokers Phillips and Drew. Stockbrokers Simon and Coates conclude that on a 'miners' strike adjusted trend' basis output has been flat and has not increased since 1983 (*Guardian*, 14 September 1984).

Growth was stimulated by the Tory government when it engineered a 'pre-election' boom to buy votes. As the *Investors' Chronicle* reported on 28 October 1983:

> The happy coincidence of all these factors – monetary expansion, scrapping hire-purchase controls in July 1982, lower interest rates, an easing of [the] fiscal stance – helps explain why growth has been faster than expected.

Increased consumer spending was helped by the abolition of hire-purchase controls. Outstanding consumer credit rose by 24 per cent between 1982 and 1983. Total household debts have risen to 60 per cent of household income (*Financial Times*, 7 February 1984).

'It is unlikely, with the savings ratio now close to 10 per cent, that private consumption will lead the rise in activity,' concludes the Bank of England's *Quarterly Bulletin* (September 1984).

When inflation starts to rise again, the Tories will cut public spending, ending the recovery. Inflation will rise to 6.5 per cent, forecasts the National Institute in its August 1984 review.

The 1984 budget

■ *On its own figures, [the budget] will not significantly reduce unemployment and it does nothing to improve the treatment of the unemployed, which is a shameful omission . . . the budget fails to deal with the fundamental problems of the economy.*
Sir Ian Gilmour, *Hansard*, 15 March 1984

In his 1984 budget speech, Chancellor Nigel Lawson predicted growth of 3 per cent in 1984. But growth is likely to be much nearer to 2 per cent. At the end of the decade, he forecast only 1.5–2 per cent growth as oil production tapers off. Even though unemployment is much higher than when Labour left office, the budget priority was still to reduce inflation.

The budget provided hardly any stimulus to the economy.

It made manufacturing investment less profitable. The proportion of the cost of new plant and machinery which can be written off against tax in the first year will be cut from 75 to 25 per cent – and that of industrial buildings from 50 to 4 per cent – by 1986. These changes will favour the service trades (which gain relatively little from capital allowances) at the expense of manufacturing industry, and companies which are not investing in new capacity at the expense of those which are. The tax burden will increase by 30 per cent for most companies, predict the Institute for Fiscal Studies (*Financial Times*, 25 June 1984).

Nigel Lawson's package also **made the poor poorer**. The increase in income tax allowances for those on low incomes is offset by inflation, increases in VAT and changes in the rules for housing benefit. The number of poor families stuck in the 'poverty trap' and forced to face marginal tax rates of 60 per cent if their income goes up will increase sixfold, warn the Institute for Fiscal Studies (*Times*, 7 April 1984).

The budget also hit:

● **Take-away food shops.** The imposition of 15 per cent VAT on hot take-away food has sent prices up (see page 121).
● **The film industry.** Because of the loss of capital allowances, as many as two-thirds of projects could go overseas or be abandoned, say the National Film Finance Corporation. This is despite the fact that Nicholas Ridley, when Financial Secretary to the Treasury, said that 100 per cent allowances for the industry would be extended until 1987 (*Financial Times*, 13 April 1984).
● **Cable TV operators.** Because capital allowances are being phased out, operators will not make a profit until their ninth

year of operation, warn accountants Deloitte Haskins and Sells. Profits had been expected in the seventh year (*Times*, 28 May 1984).

The budget changes sum up the Tory impact on the economy – the government has reduced Britain to low-wage, 'no-tech' corner shop which will only be able to sell goods designed and manufactured abroad.

Tory monetarism: no hope for the unemployed

■ *The Chancellor has no policy for unemployment save to put the entire blame on everybody but the government.*
Guardian, 10 August 1984

■ *I don't think we carry the can – and I don't think we should.*
Nigel Lawson, *Weekend World*, 21 October 1984

■ *Whether Mr Lawson likes it or not, every government has to carry the can for its actions – or lack of them.*
Daily Star editorial, 23 October 1984

Mass unemployment is an *inevitable* result of Tory monetarist policies. Governments used to believe that they had a responsibility to keep unemployment down. This one doesn't. According to Chancellor Lawson: 'It is the conquest of inflation, and not the pursuit of growth and employment, which is or should be the objective of macro-economic policy' (Mais Lecture, 18 June 1984).

The monetarist cure is very simple. Reduce inflation and unemployment will fall automatically. To reduce inflation, the money supply has to be controlled. Or that's what the Tories *used* to say. When they found out that it did not work, they claimed public borrowing had to be cut: 'fiscal policy is being rigged in the blind pursuit of a single statistic,' argued stockbrokers Laing and Cruickshank (*Guardian*, 14 February 1984).

Inflation has been reduced – but only by 1 per cent more

than the drop achieved by Britain's major competitors. The prices of food, raw materials and oil have fallen throughout the world. And wage demands have been forced down because of massive unemployment – not through some mystical link with the money supply. Monetarism has no basis in fact or theory. Despite the fall in inflation, unemployment has increased. But still the Tories pursue their monetarist theories with all the fervour of zealous ideologues. 'If we carry on with it long enough it will work. It works, it works, it works. The alternatives will not,' claimed Margaret Thatcher (*News of the World*, 20 September 1981).

MYSTERIES OF THE MONEY SUPPLY AND THE PUBLIC SECTOR BORROWING REQUIREMENT

■ *Almost all the tenets of monetarism have been destroyed.*
Sir Ian Gilmour, *Britain Can Work*, 1983

■ *The PSBR emerged from the economic wilderness in the 1970s to become one of the central pillars of economic policy. It is a bit like gauging the health of a dog by examining the size of its tail.*
Victor Keegan, *Guardian*, 28 February 1984

The government said that to get inflation down you have to hold down the money supply. But:

● A study published by the Bank of England has said that this claim is 'devoid of support'. Up to 1983, the money supply grew twice as fast as the government wanted. But inflation was falling after mid-1980.
● The various measures of the money supply (e.g. M0, M1, M3) do not move in unison. Which is the one that matters for controlling inflation? It is not clear, even to the Tories. They change the measures they try to control according to the likelihood of their targets being hit.

The government said that the way to hold down the money supply is to cut the PSBR. But:

● Studies have shown no link at all between public borrowing and money growth.
● In recent years bank lending to the UK *private* sector has been the main factor contribution to monetary growth.

The government said that cuts in borrowing would also reduce interest rates. But:

● There is no direct link between public borrowing and interest rates, concludes ex-Treasury economist Professor David Llewellyn (*Investors' Chronicle*, 17 February 1984).
● Real interest rates – interest rates after allowing for inflation – are much higher now than in 1979 when Labour left office, even though public sector borrowing has fallen as a percentage of national income. UK real interest rates in August 1984 were higher than in Germany, France and Japan, even though Britain is at the bottom of the government-borrowing league (Barclays Bank, *Financial Survey*, September 1984).

The government said that cuts in public spending were necessary to enable public borrowing and taxes to be cut. But:

● Spending cuts throw people out of work. That cuts tax revenue and pushes up spending on benefits. This automatically raises the amount the government has to borrow or means higher taxes. This is why the percentage of national income paid in taxes and national insurance contributions *rose* from 38 per cent in 1978 to 42 per cent in 1984.

Blame the unions
■ *The true British experiment is a political experiment. It is the demonstration that trade union power* can *be curbed within a free society.*

Nigel Lawson, Mais Lecture, 18 June 1984

■ *The main cause of high unemployment in Britain today – and it's much the same in the rest of Europe – is the determination*

> *of monopolistic trade unions to insist on levels of pay that price*
> *men out of work altogether.*

Nigel Lawson, 1984 Conservative Party Conference

Tory monetarism seeks to reduce inflation. But it has another, more brutal purpose. To force industry to become more efficient, firms must either innovate or liquidate. Management is encouraged to rule by fear, as mass unemployment undermines trade union organization.

The Tories are trying to force down wages by weakening unions. They claim that this will cut unemployment. In the USA, Lawson claims, jobs have been created because of the 'flexibility' of the labour market. But, as ever, there is no evidence to support his claims:

● Real wages in the USA have actually *risen* – by 4 per cent – since the end of 1982, while unemployment has *fallen* by a third.

● Britain has the *lowest* labour costs of all the major industrial countries except Spain. Yet our unemployment rate is much higher. In July 1984 the average rate of unemployment throughout the OECD was 8 per cent compared with 13 per cent in the UK.

● In Britain, unemployment among young people increased by nearly twice as much as among adults between 1979 and 1984. Yet their wages rose by 5 per cent less.

Wage-cuts may mean that labour is cheaper; but they also mean that workers have less to spend, so demand is reduced and unemployment will rise.

And wages are only one part of the total cost of British goods. The price of British exports was forced up by the overvaluation of the exchange rate in the early years of the Thatcher government and the increase in indirect taxes under the Tories.

No wonder that so many studies have disproved Lawson's claims that wage-cuts can put Britain back to work:

● *The Midland Bank Review* (Spring 1984): 'Since the end of the 1970s employment has been dropping like a stone, while the real (product) wage has been stable or even slightly falling.'

● *Gavin Davies*, chief economist at City brokers Simon and Coates: 'It is extremely difficult to discern any systematic relationship between real labour costs and employment in the UK economy' (*Financial Weekly*, August 1984).

● *Grievson Grant*, City stockbrokers: 'The current level of unemployment probably has little to do with the recent rate of real wage increase' (*Daily Mirror*, 24 October 1984).

The Tories also claim that more people would work if unemployment benefits were cut. But Britain's jobless are already worse off than those anywhere in the Western world, except Italy. An average male worker with a dependent wife and two children lost 53 per cent in income on becoming unemployed in the UK in 1982; in Denmark, France, Ireland or Holland, he would have lost just 10 per cent.

A vicious circle of decline

■ *For many years now the government has been claiming that its policies were the only ones that would create 'real' jobs. And what has been the result? Real unemployment.*

> Sir Ian Gilmour, at the London Tory Reform Group, 25 September 1984

'What the government can do to create jobs is very little indeed,' claims Lawson (*Weekend World*, 21 October 1984). But US unemployment has fallen from 11 to 7 per cent in less than two years: 'The extraordinary rate of American growth is testament to the potency of a budget stimulus,' concludes a *Guardian* editorial (10 August 1984). And this is precisely the opposite of what Lawson is doing.

The Tories' so-called 'medium-term financial strategy' traps Britain in a vicious circle of decline. Lawson wants to cut public spending to cut public borrowing. But cuts in public spending throw more people out of work, cut tax revenue, increase public spending on unemployment benefits, and worsen the financial performance of nationalized industries – forcing public borrowing to increase. This strategy means that:

● The Tories continually miss their public sector borrowing targets. In 1980, they planned to cut PSBR to just 1.5 per cent of national output by 1983–4; the actual figure was 3.25 per cent.

● Taxes have risen to record levels under the Tories. The tax burden has risen by £21 billion since 1978–9. And the share of national income taken by taxes shot up to 42 per cent in 1984, compared to 38 per cent in 1978, Labour's last year of office.

● The Tories will only be able to keep their election promise to cut taxes if they cut public spending back even further. The Tories planned tax giveaways for 1985–6 were estimated at £4 billion last year, but are now expected to be much less.

Lawson is already being forced to re-do his sums because of Britain's poor growth record. Child benefits may be taxed. Home improvement grants could be cut. And newspapers and books, tea, coffee and biscuits, could all go up in price because of VAT being imposed.

What will happen when the oil runs out?

Britain will be faced with a balance-of-payments crisis caused by its growing manufacturing trade deficit. But this is being disguised by North Sea oil revenues which now bring in £12 billion a year – £380 every second. This is equal to 9 per cent of the government's tax revenues and around 200 per cent of British manufacturing investment.

But oil revenues are starting to fall, just as Britain's manufacturing trade deficit is increasing. The National Institute and Charterhouse J. Rothschild, the financial services group, have both warned that Britain's trade could go into overall deficit in 1985.

For the first time ever in our industrial history Britain now buys more manufactured goods from abroad than it can sell overseas:

● A trade surplus in manufactured goods of £2,500 million in 1982 was turned into a trade deficit of £2,400 million in 1983 and £3,900 in 1984. Our balance on manufacturing trade worsened by £9,000 million between 1978 and 1984.

● Manufactured imports take an ever-increasing share of the British market. Their share rose by one-fifth between June 1979 and December 1983 to 31 per cent.

Table 4 Imports' share of the British market

Sector	June 1979 (%)	December 1983 (%)	Increase since June 1979 (%)
Man-made fibres	42	68	62
Motor vehicles and parts	38	51	34
Textiles	32	41	28
Metal manufacturing	25	31	23
Leather and leather goods	36	44	22
Chemicals	30	35	17
Footwear and clothing	29	34	17
Electrical and electronic engineering	37	43	16
Furniture	27	31	15
Mechanical engineering	30	33	10
Instrument engineering	56	56	0
Food, drink and tobacco	17	17	0
The whole of manufacturing industry	**25**	**31**	**23**

Source: British Business, 28 September 1984.

The decline in competitiveness can be seen in almost every sector of British industry (see Table 4). In 1983:

● The share of the British market that went to imports was: for cookers, 71 per cent; for fridges, 51 per cent; for washing machines, 44 per cent; for fridge/freezers, 35 per cent.

- Imports of colour televisions rose by half, to 35 per cent of the British market.
- British trade in commercial vehicles fell into deficit for the first time; sales of imported cars rose above 1 million for the first time, widening the deficit in cars to £2.7 billion.
- Britain's trade deficit in textiles rose by 27 per cent to a record £1,660 million; and imports of shoes took 56 per cent of the market.
- Stockbrokers Quilter Goodison forecast a deficit in engineering goods of £10,000 million by 1988.

The Tory waste of North Sea Oil revenues means that Britain is heading for a balance-of-payments crisis. Growth in Britain will be held back because any increase in demand will result in a surge in imports, says an OECD forecast (*Financial Times*, 21 June 1984). The Tories have failed to build an economy that can pay its way when the oil runs out.

Manufacturing under attack

■ *I am at a loss to understand the selective importance attached by the opposition and some Tories to the manufacturing sector.*

Nigel Lawson, House of Commons,
9 February 1984

■ *We forecast a movement into payments deficit on current account in 1985 and subsequent years . . . this highlights the need for Britain to strengthen and encourage her manufacturing industries.*

Charterhouse J. Rothschild, *Times*,
13 August 1984

Tory monetarism has made British industry less competitive than ever before. And as a result, over 1.5 million jobs have been lost in manufacturing since 1979 because:

- **Home demand has collapsed.** The Conservative

government has taken four times as much money out of the economy, through public spending cuts and tax increases, as the government of any other major country since 1980.

● **Foreign demand for British goods has been destroyed.** British goods are still about 20 per cent less price-competitive against currencies other than the dollar than in 1979.

● **Interest rates have soared.** Tory tight money policies have forced up interest rates, so businesses can't afford to invest or hold stocks.

Tory policies have turned Britain into an industrial wasteland. More and more companies are going bust. The government's lack of an industrial policy threatens the viability of key sectors. Investment in British industry is falling as companies expand overseas. We will be left without the technologies and skills needed to produce the goods and services of the 1990s.

Under the hammer

The number of business failures has soared under the Tories and continues to rise. Since 1979 there have been nearly 60,000 company liquidations and over 33,000 bankruptcies in England and Wales.

In 1984, there were almost 13,700 company liquidations – the highest number ever recorded, and three times as many as in 1979. Despite the 'recovery', there were more than 8,000 bankruptcies in 1984, some 1.7 per cent more than in 1983.

Companies which have closed down or gone into receivership since the Tories came to power range from engineering (e.g. Acrow, Alfred Herbert, Stone Platt), to microcomputers (e.g. Grundy Business Systems) to retailing (e.g. Jacksons of Piccadilly, Swan and Edgar, Biba).

Public funding cut back

Obsessed with short-term monetary targets, Tory public spending cut-backs have ignored the long-term needs of industry, both private and public:

● Public investment in industry by the government has fallen by 46 per cent in real terms over the past four years.

● Public support for aerospace, shipbuilding, steel and vehicle manufacture was cut by 80 per cent between 1982–3 and 1983–4, to just £128 million. British Leyland will get nothing from 1983–4 onwards.

● Even though nationalized industries earned a record £3,000 million overseas in 1983–4, the Tories have starved public enterprise of funding. Annual break-even targets on key industries have been imposed, which ignore their long-term needs. Since 1980–1 their 'external financing limits' – the money nationalized industries can raise from outside sources – have been slashed from £1,200 million to an estimated £142 million in 1984–5.

The Tory neglect of British industry

The Tories have abandoned key sectors, both traditional and new. They have done nothing to influence key decisions which would have helped British industry. Since the 1983 election, British Airways has bought aircraft from Boeing; Cunard has refitted the *QE2* and P&O the *Sea Princess*, in West Germany; and Dunlop Tyres was sold to the Japanese.

The sale of Dunlop shows the folly of relying on private firms – on their own – to rebuild British industry. As Andrew Alexander, the *Daily Mail*'s City editor wrote (2 May 1984):

> The whole Dunlop history of the last ten years, the mistaken European venture, the mismanagement, the cut-backs, the years in which a turn-round was forecast but did not materialize, all leave a dismal impression. I marvel at a board which, at the end of it all, wishes to crown Sir Campbell's departure with these final laurels.

Sir Campbell Fraser was given a 'golden handshake' of £120,000.

Information technology. 'It is a sunrise industry which is being eclipsed before it has even risen ... in the new industrial revolution we are falling to the point where we cannot maintain key technologies,' warned Professor John Ashworth, head of National Economic Development Office's (NEDO) information technology committee.

Not one British company is in the top ten world producers. Imports take 58 per cent of the British market, and Britain's 'real' trade deficit on information technology is £2,300 million (*Sunday Times*, 2 October 1984; *Guardian*, 7 November 1984).

Computers. ICL, Britain's leading computer manufacturer, has been sold off to Standard Telecommunications and Cables (STC) for £411 million. STC is 25 per cent owned by ITT of the USA, so technology could flow out of Britain. As Bill Johnstone, technology correspondent of the *Times* commented (17 August 1984): 'In theory, the partnership would be good for the British industry, but only if American technology does not dominate. There is every indication, however, that in the long run it will.'

Microchips. INMOS, Britain's profitable publicly owned producer of microchips, has been sold to Thorn-EMI for £95 million. The Tories had planned to sell INMOS off to the American company AT&T but had to back down in the face of public concern. But now that it is in the private sector, there is no guarantee that INMOS will receive the long-term commitment it needs.

Biotechnology. 'Britain seens to have been too half-hearted in grabbing an opportunity to take an early lead. In time-honoured fashion, it is obsessed by the pioneering technology and insufficiently alert to finance and marketing' (*Technology*, 7 May 1984).

Motors. British Leyland is soon to be denied public funding and to be privatized. Faced with fierce competition from foreign multinationals, BL may be unable to survive. It will not have sufficient funding to design and produce core components. Britain would then be without a motor manufacturer.

Japan's Nissan has been encouraged to set up an

assembly plant for putting together ready-made parts in Britain. It only has to observe a 60 per cent local-content rule, where 'local' is defined to be the EEC! 'When BL is denied access to government support by privatization, Nissan is quite likely to help itself to total control of the remnants of car-making in Britain,' warns the *Engineer* (12 January 1984).

Jaguar has been privatized. This makes no sense for either Jaguar or BL. Jaguar's recovery has been based on highly vulnerable sales to the USA. And, as Tory MP Teddy Taylor said: 'Our main fear is that if you take Jaguar out of the enterprise, BL will not be strong enough, viable enough, or glamorous enough to prosper in the future' (*Financial Times*, 28 June 1984).

Commercial vehicles. The Tories' decision to close Leyland Trucks' Bathgate plant means that Britain will no longer have an independently owned manufacturing capacity for commercial vehicles. The *Financial Times* (22 February 1984) warned that if Bathgate is closed and the Cummins engine project dropped – as has now happened – 'Leyland would have moved well down the road from being an integrated business making all its own components, to being simply an assembler of other companies' products.' But rather than invest in BL, the Tories chose to spend £15 million on redundancies at Bathgate.

Shipbuilding. 'Britain's rapidly shrinking merchant navy looks like being dealt its final death blow . . . by the Chancellor' (Victor Smart, *Observer*, 22 April 1984). The phasing-out of capital allowances, announced in the budget, will make investment unprofitable in such a capital-intensive industry. But this is no accident. Former British Shipbuilding chair, Sir Robert Atkinson, has claimed that a senior civil servant told him that 'the policy of the government is to get rid of shipbuilding altogether' (*Observer*, 12 August 1984). Moreover, British Shipbuilders will be further weakened when its warship yards are privatized. It will have to compete with those yards for Ministry of Defence orders.

Investment crisis

British industry needs to invest in modern technologies if it is to have any chance of competing in world markets. Industry's investment record was already poor before the Tories came to power. Since then, investment by firms in British manufacturing has fallen further while companies have expanded overseas:

- Manufacturing investment has fallen by 25 per cent since 1979.
- From 1979 to 1982, investment in British manufacturing was not even sufficient to replace worn-out plant and machinery.
- Dunlop, Courtaulds, Lucas, Vickers, Rank Hovis McDougall, Thorn-EMI, Rolls Royce, Vauxhall, Tube Investments and British Shipbuilders all invested less than £1,000 per worker in 1982–3. (*Labour Research*, May 1984).

Many companies have dished out extra dividends to shareholders, rather than reinvest in their business. 'Uncovered' dividends (payments to shareholders not covered by company earnings) went up from 34 per cent in 1979 to 36 per cent in 1981.

The trend of high dividends for shareholders is set to continue. The London Business School forecasts that over the four years to 1987, dividends on companies' ordinary shares will rise in real terms by 22 per cent, while companies' fixed investment will show a recovery of only 15 per cent (*Economic Outlook*, February 1984).

Other companies have built up 'cash mountains' rather than invest. 'Lex', the influential column of the *Financial Times*, (5 August 1984) describes this policy as 'the badge of an excessively cautious management'. The GEC 'mountain' alone stands at £1,350 million.

Multinational merry-go-round

British-based multinationals have expanded overseas. The top 50 British manufacturers increased their overseas production by 24 per cent between 1980 and 1982. And while their UK workforce fell by nearly 0.5 million, their non-UK workforce rose.

The Tories want to attract multinationals. Government policies of low wages and curbing union rights are 'incentives' for foreign companies to invest in Britain, according to *Multinational Investment Strategies in the British Isles* (HMSO, 1983).

Capital flight

The Tories scrapped exchange controls just five months after their return to office. The result has been a bonanza in UK private overseas investment as nearly £50,000 million flowed out of the country from 1979–83:

● Annual UK private investment overseas rose from £4,600 million in 1978 to no less than £10,600 million in 1983.

● Of this, investment by UK financial institutions in foreign companies jumped from £0.9 million in 1979 to £6,100 million in 1983.

There is no guarantee that the earnings from abroad will be reinvested in Britain, says a study by the American Express Bank: 'The UK will have to compete for these resources along with the rest of the world.'

The Tories claim that they have made Britain more attractive for foreign investors and that this offsets the flight of capital abroad. But total foreign investment in the UK rose from only £1,900 million in 1978 to £5,400 million in 1983. Most of this was due to North Sea Oil – little went into British manufacturing.

Future shock

■ *Whoever controls the technology controls the wealth of tomorrow. Those who make the products will also control the flow of wealth throughout the world.*

Richard Sharpe, Editor of *Computing Times*, 4 September 1984

■ *Draw any industrial league table, and Britain is going to be at or near the bottom of it.*

Engineer, 3 May 1984

The failure to finance British industry

Banks don't provide enough long-term finance on the right terms and conditions, says a 1983 report by the Fellowship of Engineering. *Modern Materials in Manufacturing Industry* goes on to argue that long-term finance is vital, because innovations (such as carbon fibres) can take up to ten years to develop. Financial institutions are also technically ignorant, says the report.

The failure to invest

Britain's failure to invest means that our industry has outdated technologies, and is unable to produce modern goods and services:

● For every robot installed in Britain, West Germany has invested in three and Japan in eight. (*Technology*, 22 August 1983).

● Half of Britain's factories do not use microelectronics in their production processes, and have no plans to do so in the future. The recession and lack of experience are the main obstacles, is the conclusion reached by the Policy Studies Institute's *Microelectronics in British Industry*, March 1984.

● Almost three-quarters of British engineering outfits don't even have access to a computer (*Technology*, 11 June 1984). A NEDO report concludes that at least £4 billion would be freed from Britain's stock and work in progress for reinvestment if stock management was as good in Britain as it is in the USA or West Germany (*Technology*, 23 July 1984).

The failure to innovate

There is no shortage of new ideas in Britain. Fifty-five per cent of the world's most significant inventions since 1945 have come from Britain, says a report by the Ministry of International Trade and Industry (MITI) in Japan (*Engineer*,

12 July 1984). But we have no mechanism for exploiting them. The main problems of British industry 'lie in its failure to up-date design and in its failure to grasp the importance of science and technology to competititiveness', concludes a report by the International Labour Organization (*Financial Times*, 10 February 1984).

Those countries that spend most on innovation have the largest share of world exports and are more likely to keep imports down. But British companies don't give enough priority to innovation and the Tories have failed to finance research:

● Two-fifths of British companies have no strategy for innovation and the use of new technology – twice as many as in Belgium – a survey by MORI found (*Engineer*, 3 May 1984).

● Britain spends less on industrial research and development – and more on defence – than almost all our major competitors. Despite this, large British firms have actually cut their research and development budgets during the recession, concludes the Technical Change Centre (*New Techology*, 24 September 1984).

● The Science and Engineering Research Council – the main promoter of high technology research – hasn't got enough money to support all the high-priority projects it has been asked to assist (*Technology*, 3 September 1984). Spending cuts have forced the Department of Trade and Industry to freeze a scheme to strengthen links between industry and academic institutions (*Financial Times*, 18 July 1984).

The failure to train
Britain has one of the most poorly trained workforces in the world:

● The percentage of the British workforce with recognized qualifications is no more than half that of the USA, Japan and West Germany, concludes the Institute of Manpower Studies in its 'fierce indictment of Britain's record on industrial training' (*Sunday Times*, 25 August 1984).

● Britain's engineering industries will take on only half of the 13,000 apprentices they need, warns the Engineering Industry Training Board. Money from the MSC is going to provide cheap replacements for apprentices on the YTS, not into apprenticeship schemes (*Engineer*, 5 July 1984).

British industry is being held back because of skill shortages. Companies can't get hold of adequately trained staff to take advantage of their new investment, concludes a survey by Works Management (*Financial Times*, 31 July 1984). British high-technology industries could lose about £2 billion a year in home and overseas sales by 1990 because of the growing skills crisis, predicts the trade magazine *Technology* (7 March 1983).

The sale of the century

■ *As Mrs Thatcher's housewifely economics might have it, the government is selling off the family heirlooms to pay the grocery bills.*

> *Times* editorial, 26 July 1983

The Conservative government plans to sell off public assets worth £10 billion during the next five years (*Financial Times*, 28 January 1984). Its privatization programme is set out on pages 101–2.

Privatization of these vital assets will be bad for Britain for two main reasons:

● First, it will reduce government income in the long term. The Tories want to use the sale of these assets to fund income tax cuts. But the cut in government revenue will mean that future governments will be forced to increase *indirect* taxes or cut spending, in order to sustain tax cuts.

● Second, many of the companies that have been sold off are of vital strategic importance. So privatization further weakens the British economy.

The Tories claim that the 'sell-off' spreads share

ownership: 'the truest public ownership of all,' they claimed in their election manifesto. But about two-thirds of the shares that have been sold off are now owned by the big financial institutions, over which members of the public have no control.

THE PRIVATIZATION PROGRAMME

What's gone

Year	Sale	Amount (£m)
1979–80	5 per cent of BP	276
	25 per cent of ICL	37
	Shares in Suez Finance Company and other miscellaneous	57
1980–1	50 per cent of Ferranti	55
	100 per cent of Fairey	22
	North Sea oil licences	195
	51 per cent of British Aerospace	43
	Miscellaneous and small NEB holdings	91
1981–2	24 per cent of British Sugar	44
	50 per cent of Cable and Wireless	182
	100 per cent of Amersham	64
	100 per cent of National Freight Corporation	5
	Crown Agent and Forestry Commission land and property sales and other miscellaneous	199
1982–3	51 per cent of Britoil (first cash call)	334
	49 per cent of Associated British Ports	46
	British Transport Hotels	40
	International Aeradio	60
	Sale of oil licences, oil stockpiles and miscellaneous	108
1983–4	Second cash call, Britoil	293

Year	Sale	Amount (£m)
	7 per cent of BP	565
	25 per cent of Cable and Wireless	260
1984–5	JH Sankey	12
	Scott Lithgow	12
	Lye Tinplate	16
	100 per cent of Enterprise Oil	392
	50 per cent of Wytch Farm	215
	48.5 per cent of Associated British Ports	51
	76 per cent of INMOS	95
	Sealink	66
	Jaguar	297
	British Telecom (first of three cash calls)	1,300
	Total	**5,432**

What's Going*

Year	Sale	Amount (£m)
	British Airways	800
1985–6	British Telecom (second call)	1,300
	British Airports	400
	11 Royal Ordnance factories	400
1985–6	British Telecom (third call)	1,300
1986–7	Some parts gas, electricity, plus about £1 billion of smaller enterprises including National Bus, Land Rover, Rolls Royce, Unipart, British Steel profitable businesses, British Nuclear Fuels, naval shipbuilding yards.	4,700
	Further tranches of BP and BT might also be sold.	
	Total	**8,400**

*Figures are working assumptions.
Sources: Financial Times, 7 February 1984: *Observer*, 15 July 1984; *Guardian*, 23 October 1984.

- **British Aerospace** about 75 per cent of shares are held by 197 major institutions.
- **Cable and Wireless** 75 per cent of shares are held by 467 major institutions. Only 5 per cent of shares are held by small investors – those with less than 1,000 shares.
- **Amersham International** 69 per cent of shares are held by 102 large shareholders.
- **Britoil** 82 per cent of shares are held by 383 large shareholders (*Labour Research*, September 1984).

The sale of British Telecom (BT) shares has increased share ownership. But only because of the massive advertising campaign costing £50 million and the giveaway terms of the sale. The shares were heavily under-priced (see pages 108–9) and £113 million will be given away in vouchers and bonus shares. In addition, the government took the unethical step of paying commissions to banks, stockbrokers and other financial advisers who submitted applications on behalf of their clients.

Even the executive director of the Bank of England, David Walker, believes that Tory plans for wider share ownership are 'unrealistic in the foreseeable future', because the tax system favours institutions owning shares and because individual share ownership may not be the best way for small shareholders to hold wealth (*Guardian*, 3 November 1984).

The Tories also claim that the public sector is unproductive and a burden on British industry. By transferring companies to the private sector, they argue, companies will become more efficient because they will have to compete: 'State ownership should be displaced or supplemented, wherever sensibly possible, by the discipline and pressures of the marketplace and by some degree of private ownership,' Sir Geoffrey Howe has claimed (Conservative Party Summer School, 3 July 1982).

This is nonsense. Even some Tory MPs, such as Sir Ian Gilmour, have admitted as much:

There is a presumption, I think, that industries are

better run in private hands than in public. But that is not a universally known truth for all times and places and for all industries. (*Hansard*, 16 January 1984).

The growth of the private sector depends on a healthy public sector. Each year the public sector buys £13 billion of total manufacturing output; four-fifths of all goods bought by the government are produced in the private sector. The public sector creates wealth and it provides the infrastructure of services, such as transport and energy, which are vital to Britain's economy.

Companies like British Airways and British Leyland have become more efficient through public investment and better management while under *public* ownership.

Many of the companies which are being sold off will still be monopolies. British Airways will have 62 per cent of the domestic market – a lower share might have cut future profits and threatened privatization. British Telecom will also be a monopoly. Even Lord Weinstock of GEC was forced to argue:

I am not clear what point there is in privatizing a company which is by nature a monopoly. I don't see how you can have anything other than a monopoly running a national communication service. (*Guardian*, 15 July 1983).

The truth is that public assets are being sold off at knockdown prices to pay for the Tory government's mis-handling of the economy. As Nigel Lawson put it: 'Although the purpose of privatization is to have a more effective, more efficient, more competitive and more dynamic economy, *there are benefits to the Treasury along the road* (*Hansard*, 27 October 1983, our emphasis).

The government has had to raise money in this way because it has got its sums wrong. When the Conservative government announced its decision to sell £500 million extra British Petroleum shares, a leader in the Times (26 July 1983) scathingly referred to 'the legitimate suspicion that the

Chancellor is taking easy short-term measures to disguise long-term budgetary problems and delay action to resolve them'.

In their rush to make money, assets have been sold off at knockdown prices. The taxpayer has already lost over £2,300 million (see pages 108–9).

Both the Public Accounts Committee, a key House of Commons watchdog body, and the Royal Institute of Public Administration have accused the government of mishandling the sale of public assets (*Financial Times*, 14 June 1984; *Guardian*, 15 October 1984).

So badly has the sell-off been managed that the 'Lex' column in the *Financial Times* (29 June 1984) wrote, when the Tories sold off shares in Enterprise Oil, that 'Mr Peter Walker managed in a few minutes yesterday to create as much ill-will as some Labour governments have achieved in an entire term of office.'

The 'piratization' of British Telecom

■ *All that will occur is that BT will gain greater access to private finance while losing what little public accountability it had. That is not competition; it is corporatism.*

Times editorial, 18 July 1983

■ *We have been engaged . . . in creating the most enormous private monopoly and monolith out of what is already a public monopoly.*

Tory MP Peter Temple-Morris, *Hansard*, 18 July 1983

The government claims that privatizing BT will benefit consumers by bringing down prices and increasing efficiency. But:

● The prices charged by BT, while *publicly* owned, were among the lowest in the world. Prices were 60 per cent higher in West Germany, for example. And BT telephone waiting lists fell from 200,000 to 2,000 in the past three years.

• Prices of key services will rocket after privatization. BT will be required to limit price rises to 3 per cent less than the rate of inflation. But this restriction covers only 62 per cent of BT turnover. The Post Office Users' National Council has described these arrangements as 'totally inadequate'. Call-box rates and residential rental charges could rise far faster than in the past (*Financial Times*, 4 May 1984).

Already, major price increases have been announced, from November 1984 onwards: quarterly rentals and call unit charges *up* 7 per cent; minimum payphone charges *up* 100 per cent – from 5p to 10p.

• Many services are threatened by privatization: public call boxes, emergency services, rural services, enquiries and information services, help for the disabled, and the low-user rebate. And the licence makes no demand that the quality of service be improved.

The threat to prices and services exists because investors will buy shares only if they can see a profit. This profit can only come from the abuse of BT's monopoly powers over residential and other services, as the private monopoly jacks up prices and cuts back on loss-making services. The pressure to do this will increase because BT has to compete with its new rival, Mercury, for business services, which generate much of BT's income.

The government has set up 'Oftel' to regulate BT. But it will have less than half the staff of the body established to monitor New York's phone service. And in New York, unlike Britain, customers can make their views known in public hearings, and there are clear and legally enforceable codes of conduct, including rights of redress for customers and fines for non-compliance. In the words of Alex Henney, chair of the London Electricity Consumer Council: 'We are setting up an enormous private monopoly that is unaccountable, under-regulated and largely unassailable' (*Financial Times*, 7 March 1984).

Privatization of BT will also be a disaster for British industry and jobs. It will result in a surge in imports and the loss of jobs, because a privately owned BT will be free to buy abroad. BT currently buys 95 per cent of its products in the UK, providing orders for 70,000 jobs. The Tories' own 'Think Tank' has produced a report which aims for a reduction of 45,000 jobs in BT.

It is in this context – of higher prices, poorer services, and the threat to jobs and British industry – that selling shares in BT to small investors and employees must be judged.

Shareholders had to buy at least £260-worth of shares. But they only paid about £100 at the start – the rest will be bought on credit. They are entitled to up to 12 vouchers, worth £18, which can be used to pay telephone bills and are free from income tax. Alternatively, they are entitled to receive one bonus share for every ten they have purchased.

But many small shareholders are expected to sell out in a year's time, when they have cashed in their vouchers. If they do this it will force down the price of BT shares. Other shareholders may also want to sell their shares if this happens.

BT workers were given the option to accept £70-worth of shares free, a further bonus of £200 if they subscribed for £100-worth, and further discounts on purchases up to £2,000 in value. But many will lose their jobs.

However many people have shares in BT, it will inevitably be *controlled* by the major City institutions, which will buy up the shares sold off by small investors. The institutions have already benefitted from the increase in the value of BT shares on the day it was sold off – an increase of £1,300. And they will be attracted by the high profits – of more than 17 per cent – that can be made from BT shares by exploiting BT's monopoly power.

BT shows what happens when private profit is put before efficient service to the community. Private capital will gain control over telecommunications, a vital strategic sector of the future. Other countries would not take the risk of selling shares in this vital sector to foreign capital. The Japanese, for instance, have a law making this impossible.

That is the harsh political truth concealed by an advertising campaign costing £50 million, which persuaded people to buy what they *already* owned.

The Tories look after City friends

Privatization handouts

City speculators are making huge profits from the Tories' sale of public assets at knockdown prices, while taxpayers are estimated to have lost over £2,300 million. When BT was privatized, the value of its shares rose by nearly £1,300 million by the end of the first day of trading (see Table 5). The Wytch Farm oilfield was valued by British Gas at three times the price at which it was sold off, according to the Royal Institute for Public Administration (*Guardian*, 15 October 1984).

Table 5   Losses on sales of public assets

Company	Date	Sale price (p)	Share price since sell-off (p)		Government loss (£m)[a]
			high	low	
British Aerospace	Feb. 1981	150	401	170	251
Cable & Wireless	Oct. 1981	168	387	191	291
Amersham International	Feb. 1982	142	303	186	161
Britoil	Nov. 1982	215	277	157[b]	158
Associated British Ports	Feb. 1983	112	298	129	36
Cable & Wireless	Dec. 1983	275	387	270[b]	112
Associated British Ports	April 1984	270	298	272	5
Jaguar	Aug. 1984	165	179[c]		25
British Telecom	Nov. 1984	50[d]	93[c]		1,295
Total loss					**2,334**

Notes:
[a] Based on highest price since sale of shares times the number of shares sold.
[b] Since shares were fully paid for.
[c] Price at end of first day's dealing.
[d] Partly paid price; full price of £1.30 to be paid by April 1986.
Sources: Labour Research, September 1984; *Financial Times*, 4 December 1984.

108

City bankers and advisers had collected £30 million in privatization fees by July 1984. But this was dwarfed by the £128 million they subsequently received from the BT sale (*Hansard*, 28 November 1984).

City lifeboat
When Johnson Matthey Bankers (JMB), the gold bullion bank, was on the verge of collapse the Bank of England stepped in and took it into public ownership. Two issues are raised by the JMB affair:

- **Double standards.** The JMB rescue contrasts sharply with Tory insistence on closing unprofitable pits despite the devastating social and economic effects of closures on mining communities. The Tories apply one set of principles to the City and another to industry.
- **Inadequate supervisory procedures.** The procedures by which the Bank of England supervises banks are governed by the Banking Act 1979 and rely heavily on honesty and co-operation. The main reason why the Bank of England did not foresee problems coming sooner at JMB was because information on doubtful loans had not been disclosed.

City poodles or bloodhounds?
Proposals for a new framework for investor protection were outlined by the government in October 1984. Rather than opting for a strong independent securities commission to supervise the City's finance markets, the government decided that the new structure is to be firmly based on the principle of *self-regulation*. One or two co-ordinating umbrella bodies are to be established; beneath these will be a number of self-regulating agencies.

The co-ordinating bodies are to be set up and financed by the City itself, so there are widespread fears that the new bodies will prove ineffective watchdogs. As the *Financial Times* (18 October 1984) said: 'The threat is that the new agencies will turn out to be captives of the interests which they are supposed to regulate.'

A major weakness of the proposals is that no attempt has

been made to tackle the problem of regulating the expanding market in Eurobonds – the market for bonds denominated in currencies other than those of the country in which they are issued. This huge market has recently exploded. It was described by Professor Gower, who headed the government review of investor protection, as 'virtually unregulated', and by the chair of the Stock Exchange as 'failing in honesty'. Regulation would require co-ordinated international action. But .as the *Guardian* (18 October 1984) remarked: 'Until it happens, there must be a feeling that the government is merely shutting the safe-door after the bonds have bolted.'

Britain's abandoned regions

■ *This marks the effective end of regional policy as we have known it.*

> Geoffrey Robinson, Labour's regional spokesperson, commenting on regional-aid cuts, *Labour Weekly*, 7 December 1984

The regional problem has worsened during the recession. Unemployment in the North has risen to 19 per cent, compared to 10 per cent in the South-east.

Employment has fallen faster in all the areas which have traditionally been eligible for regional assistance than in the non-assisted areas, with only two exceptions (Scotland, an assisted area where employment has fallen more slowly; and the West Midlands, which was until recently a non-assisted area, where employment has fallen faster).

That's what happens when growth is left to 'market forces'. Tory regional 'policy' has been an excuse for spending cuts, of almost one-third between 1982–3 and 1983–4 – from nearly £920 million to under £650 million. These cuts have been condemned by the Tory-dominated Commons Welsh Affairs Select Committee (*Financial Times*, 25 May 1984), by accountants Deloitte, Haskins and Sells (*Financial Times*, 5 June 1984), and by the Association of British Chambers of Commerce (*Financial Times*, 18 July 1984).

Further sharp cuts in regional aid were announced in November 1984, following the government's review of regional policy. By 1987–8, spending will be reduced by £300 million – a cut of 50 per cent. Special Development Area status, which was granted to the most needy areas, will be abolished.

Conservative 'reforms' have already made regional policy less effective. Regional Selective Assistance, the main method of job creation, has been halved since 1978. A quarter of total selective aid to industry now goes to firms in the South-east.

The Tories' 1984 White Paper *Regional Industrial Development* offers nothing to the regions, except further spending cuts. Rightly, it argues that spending has not been effective in terms of job creation – but this is an argument for making sure that *current* spending is better used, not for cutting it back even further.

The best way to create jobs in the regions, claim the Tories, is to cut wages. But this is nonsense, both at the national and regional levels. In areas of Britain where wages have grown *faster* than the national average, unemployment has risen *less*. In the West Midlands, between 1967 and 1982 earnings fell by 9.5 per cent compared with the rest of Britain – but unemployment rose by 20 per cent more than elsewhere.

The Tories' regional policy completely fails to address the key issues vital to regional recovery. High-unemployment regions all have highly vulnerable economies, dominated by branch plants of major companies. These plants last only a few years before they are closed down. The Tories offer nothing that will build up the regions' own capacity for industrial growth.

Instead, the Tories have promoted Enterprise Zones, which offer a massive property subsidy in the form of complete rate relief for a ten-year period, together with other benefits. Their record suggests that the enterprise they have encouraged is anything but 'free':

● The 8,065 jobs created in the first 11 enterprise zones cost £132.9 million, at a cost of £16,478 per job, according to a report by Roger Tym and Partners (*Monitoring Enterprise Zones*, January 1984).

● The zones have failed to create additional employment. Three out of every four companies came from the same county and at least 85 per cent originated within the same region. The main 'achievement' of the zones has been to redistribute employment.

● The *Investors' Chronicle* (8 July 1983) concludes, 'The simple fact is that there is no proven track record to far that Enterprise Zones actually do create employment.'

The Tories have also set up six 'free ports' – areas to which goods can be imported free of customs duties provided they are sent abroad after processing. These are in Belfast, Birmingham, Cardiff, Liverpool, Prestwick and Southampton. The government has caved in to business pressure in establishing so many. 'The only places that make real commercial sense are Southampton and Aberdeen and one of those has been excluded,' said one industrialist associated with the 'free port' application (*Financial Times*, 3 February 1984).

Britain's inner cities have been abandoned to private speculators and philanthropy. Urban policy is now just an excuse for subsidizing property and site development. Inner City Enterprises was set up by Michael Heseltine after the inner-city riots of 1981 as a 'broker' to seek out private funding for large inner-city projects. Its first annual report shows that it has not yet attracted a single funding agreement (*Financial Times*, 25 July 1984).

A 'shoeshine' economy

■ *All our competitors are moving into new industries, but the British Chancellor wants his country to become a 'shoeshine' economy.*

Neil Kinnock, *Hansard*, 30 October 1984

■ *Many of the jobs of the future will be in labour-intensive*

service industries which are not so much low-tech as no-tech.
Nigel Lawson, speaking to the International Monetary
Fund, 25 September 1984

The Tories have failed to build an economy that can pay its way when the oil runs out. There is nothing accidental about this. They are turning Britain into the corner shop of the industrial world – a trading-post for foreign producers, unable to provide the goods and services of the future.

British industry has been left to rot as money floods overseas; public assets have been squandered as the City has made a killing; the rights of working people have been treated with contempt as mass unemployment has been used to control trade unions and curb wage demands.

But the treatment is killing the patient: British industry has become less competitive than ever before. Instead of investing in modern technologies and skills, the Tories have wasted £29,000 million of North Sea oil revenues to finance a spending spree on imports, tax cuts for the rich, and benefits for the unemployed.

3. Robbing the poor

Wealth distribution: Tories reverse 60-year trend

The distribution of wealth in Britain is very unequal. In 1982 the wealthiest **1 per cent of the people owned one-fifth of the total wealth**; the richest 10 per cent owned more than half. The poorest half of the population owned just 4 per cent of the wealth.

● More than half of the adult population had less than £5,000-worth of wealth.
● The wealthiest 5 per cent each owned assets worth more than £50,000.

The government claims it wants to spread wealth more equally. Yet the Tories have managed to reverse a 60-year trend towards more equal distribution of wealth. Between 1980 and 1982 the richest 5 per cent of the population increased their share of the wealth from 38 per cent to 41 per cent; the share owned by the poorest 75 per cent fell from 24 per cent to 19 per cent.

Tory tax policies are scandalously favourable to the wealthy. **In 1980–81, 18 people died leaving more than £1 million without paying a penny in tax.** Nearly 600 people left more than £200,000 without paying any tax. The Tories have:

● Abolished the investment income surcharge for the benefit of those with an income from investment of more than £7,100 a year – which normally requires having assets, other than a home or personal possessions, of at least £70,000.
● Cut the top tax rate on investment income from 98 to 60 per cent, and the top rate on earnings from 83 to 60 per cent.

• Neutered capital transfer tax whose top rate was cut from 75 per cent in 1979 to 60 per cent, and to only 30 per cent on lifetime gifts. The tax charged used to be based on the cumulation of transfers over a lifetime; now it depends only on transfers made over the previous ten years. There is also generous provision for the payment of capital transfer tax by instalments.

As the *Investors' Chronicle* (7 January 1983) has pointed out: 'Capital transfer tax is becoming an avoidable tax, and with the many relaxations in capital gains tax that also is having much less impact.'

Income gap widens

Unequal shares

The distribution of income has become even more unequal under the Tories. Between 1978–9 and 1981–2 the share of after tax income earned by the poorest half of the population fell from 27 per cent to 25 per cent, while the share earned by the top 20 per cent rose from 40 per cent to 42 per cent (*Economic Trends*, July 1984). The richest 10 per cent increased their disposable income in real terms by £1,557 a year between 1978–9 and 1981–2, whereas the poorest 20 per cent became £82 a year poorer. In 1981–2 the average post-tax income for all households was £5,020, compared with £22,840 for the top 10 per cent and £1,630 for the bottom 20 per cent. (Peter Townsend, 'Why are the Many Poor', 1984.)

Directors profit . . .

The gap between the pay of company directors and manual workers has widened, according to a survey by *Labour Research* (November 1984). The survey showed that:

• In 1979, the 20 highest-paid directors together received as much as 454 average male manual workers. By 1983, they were paid more than 722 such workers – a total of £5.5 million between them.

• The number of company directors being paid over

£100,000 a year more than doubled between 1982 and 1983 to 179. The highest-paid was Richard Giordano of British Oxygen Corporation who received £521,500 a year.

● Forty men received over £0.25 million from their companies in pay and dividends in 1983. Top places went to the Sainsbury supermarket family. David Sainsbury, finance director of the chain, received over £5.5 million in 1983. His cousin, Timothy Sainsbury, and brother, John, picked up £1.8 million and £2 million respectively. The three of them have received an average *increase* of almost £0.5 million since 1983.

Company executives' fringe benefits have grown considerably over the last five years, according to a survey by the Inbucon management consultancy. Between 1978 and 1984 the percentage of managers given full use of a company car, for example, rose from 67 per cent to 78 per cent; the percentage receiving life assurance of over three times their salary rose from 27 per cent to 42 per cent.

. . . While wages of the poorest are forced down

The Tories claim that poverty wages will price workers into jobs. They are using mass unemployment, backed by anti-union legislation, to force down wages. Other measures include:

● Repeal of Schedule II of the Employment Protection Act, which gave workers the right to arbitration and fair wages.
● Abolition of the Clegg Comparability Commission, which compared pay in the public services with the private sector.
● Scrapping of the Pay Research Unit, which compared civil servants' pay with pay in the private sector.
● Repeal of the Fair Wages Resolution, which guaranteed fair wages for those employed under government contracts.
● Ordering District Health Authorities to put ancillary services out to tender to private contractors.
● Introducing the Young Workers Scheme, which offers a subsidy to employers if, and only if, they pay low wages to the young people they employ.

The government is also considering the abolition of Wages Councils. These bodies set a legal minimum wage for nearly 3 million low-paid workers in services and manufacturing jobs. But the rates set are extremely low:

● The minimum rate of pay for an adult working as a hairdressing shampooist, for example, is £47.50 for a 40-hour week. A fully qualified hairdresser, after five years' training, is entitled to just £64.80 for 40 hours.
● The highest rates currently set by the Wages Councils are still below £80 a week for non-management staff, or less than half of the average adult wage.

Even the Confederation of British Industry does not favour complete abolition of Wages Councils, recognizing that 'a safety-net was still needed for low-paid groups of workers' (CBI evidence to the House of Commons Select Committee on Employment, 1984). But this government is intent on bringing down the wages of the poorest.

The Tories' policies have resulted in a massive rise in the number of low-paid workers:

● The proportion of male manual workers who are low-paid (where low pay is defined to be 68 per cent of average male earnings, or £108.30 a week in 1984) has doubled; one in ten earned less than this in 1979, compared with one in five in 1984. Among women manual workers the proportion has risen from two-thirds to four-fifths over the same period. This level of earnings would leave a single person with a disposable income of just £7.54 a day for *all needs* excluding housing and work expenses, and would leave a family of four with a daily income of only £2.43 per person.
● On Merseyside, one-quarter of all people in full-time work earn less than £100 per week, according to the Low Pay Unit. The proportion rises to nearly one-third when overtime is excluded. Some workers on Merseyside are receiving very low wages indeed – for example, there are full-time office workers on £30 per week and security guards earning an average of £1 per hour for a 110-hour week (*Guardian*, 27 September 1984).

Breadline Britain

After just two years of Thatcher's government, **nearly 4 million people had been added to the ranks of the poor.** In 1981:

● 15 million people – over a quarter of the population – were living on incomes no more than 40 per cent above supplementary benefit rates, the level generally regarded as the poverty line. This compares with just over 11 million people in 1979.
● 2.8 million of them were living on incomes below supplementary benefit rates – almost 0.75 million more than in 1979.

Since then, the numbers in poverty have undoubtedly increased. During 1981 nearly 5 million people were living on supplementary benefit. By December 1983 this number had risen to an appalling 7.2 million.

Poverty used to be a problem mainly of the elderly. Now there are more people under pension age than over living in poverty. The creation of mass unemployment, in particular the emergence of long-term unemployment, cuts in national insurance benefits and the increasing incidence of low pay are the major factors in this explosion of poverty:

● The number of people living in poverty as a result of unemployment has more than trebled since 1979.
● In 1981 almost 4 million people were living in or on the margins of poverty, even though they were in families with at least one full-time earner – about 50 per cent more than in 1979.

In Thatcher's Britain, more and more children are being brought up in poverty.

● In 1981 almost 3.75 million children were living in or on the margins of poverty – more than a quarter of the children in this country, and over 1.25 million more than in 1979.
● Over 0.5 million of these children were living in families whose income was below supplementary benefit rates – almost double the number in 1979.

A MORI poll for the television series *Breadline Britain* revealed what poverty meant for people in Britain in 1983:

- 3.25 million people can't afford to heat their homes adequately;
- 4.3 million people live in damp housing conditions;
- 3.4 million people can't afford all the food they would like;
- 6 million people have been in serious arrears with essential bills in the past year;
- 10 million people can't afford even a week's holiday.

Trapped into poverty

■ *We shall . . . reduce the poverty trap.*

Conservative manifesto, 1979

The Tories have cut tax rates for the rich but they have increased them for the poor. The poverty trap has tightened its grip around more and more people as the direct result of government policies. The poverty trap results from the overlap of means-tested benefits and taxation; it means that for every £1 wage increase, at least 75p is taken away in tax and the loss of means-tested benefits – so making it impossible for low-paid families to earn their way out of poverty. A series of government measures – in particular, the abolition in 1980 of the reduced rate of income tax, increases in the family income supplement limits and increases in the rate at which housing benefit is withdrawn as income rises – has extended the poverty trap to more families:

- The number of families in the poverty trap has trebled in the five years 1979–84, to 270,000.
- Nearly nine out of ten families considered poor enough to claim family income supplement now pay tax, compared to six out of ten in 1978.

In the March 1984 budget, Nigel Lawson claimed that raising personal allowances would 'ease the poverty trap'. But:

- Of the 850,000 people taken out of the tax net by the budget

changes, only 10,000 were families caught in the poverty trap.
● The April and November 1984 changes in housing benefit
have worsened the poverty trap.

Nigel Lawson should listen to his own Treasury officials.
In evidence to the House of Commons Treasury Select
Committee, George Monger, an Under-Secretary at the
Treasury, said: 'It would take a long haul to solve the poverty
trap by raising personal allowances.' A substantial increase in
child benefit would be much more effective – but the
government will make no commitment on that.

Prices

Back in 1979 the Tories, in their manifesto, said that one of
the five tasks of their government was: 'To restore the health
of our economic and social life by controlling inflation.'
   **The Tories sent inflation soaring in their first year,
more than doubling the rate from 10 to 22 per cent.** The
increase in VAT alone added nearly 4 per cent to prices.
Prices of goods and services produced by nationalized
industries were forced up by more than the increase in the
rate of inflation. Rents, rates and interest rates were all hiked.
Moreover, one of the Tories' first measures was to abolish the
Price Commission, which had checked prices under Labour.
   **Since the Tories came to power, prices have risen
by 66 per cent.** The Tory pound is now worth just 58 pence.
The rate of inflation has now fallen to around 5 per cent. But
the overall reduction in inflation under the Tories is only 1
percentage point more than the decrease experienced by our
major competitors over the same period. Inflation has
declined throughout the world because of falling commodity
prices. The cost of achieving the extra reduction in the UK
has been huge – 4 million on the dole and British industry in
tatters: so much for restoring the health of our economy.
   Nor should we forget that the impact of price increases has
fallen most heavily on the less well-off members of society.
Thus, while on average prices have risen by 66 per cent:

- The cost of housing, fuel and light has doubled.
- The rise in prices for the low-paid, as calculated by the Low Pay Unit, has been 4 per cent above the average.

And for a government which claims to be so committed to controlling price rises, the Tories have adopted some remarkably strange policies. They have:

- Doubled VAT. A move which helped to more than double the rate of inflation in the space of a year.
- Slapped VAT on take-away foods. A move which resulted in 14,000 lost jobs and a 20 per cent drop in turnover.
- Insisted that nationalized industries, against their better judgement, increase their prices above the rate of inflation.
- Agreed, year in, year out, to unacceptable increases in Common Market food prices, despite the massive surpluses and the falling demand for food.
- Maintained a tax on UK food – sometimes as high as 18 per cent – by refusing to devalue the 'green pound'.

And everything points to bigger price rises in the near future:

- Sterling has plummeted – forcing up the cost of imports.
- Interest rates have shot up – back to the near-record levels they were when the Tories pushed inflation up to 22 per cent.
- Electricity prices are due to soar – as a result of Tory intransigence over the coal strike.
- Factory-gate and raw-material prices are rising faster than the rate of inflation – an early warning of the bad times ahead.
- All the indications are that the VAT base is to be extended possibly to include food, newspapers, books and fuel. If VAT was put on all the items currently zero-rated it would more than double the present rate of inflation.

Tory claims on prices are bogus. They have tried to con the British people: they have neither controlled price rises *nor* restored health to our economy.

Record taxes

■ *We shall cut income tax at all levels.*

Conservative manifesto, 1979

■ *We have had over the past four years to increase the level of taxation overall.*

Nigel Lawson, *Financial Times*, 7 September 1983

Since 1979 the tax burden has increased for most people. But the increase has been borne disproportionately by the poor.

● The total tax burden rose from 38 per cent of Gross Domestic Product in 1979 to 43 per cent in 1984.
● Since 1979 the tax burden has increased for all income groups. But the highest-paid 10 per cent paid 3 per cent *less* of their incomes in tax in 1981–2 than in 1978–9.

Tax concessions to the rich since 1979 are worth £3 billion per year, as Table 6 shows. Taxation for ordinary families has been increased by:
● virtually doubling the VAT rate, from 8 to 15 per cent in 1979.
● Increasing employees' national insurance contribution rates in 1980, 1981 and 1982, which, for most families, wiped out the benefit of the 3p-in-the-pound cut in the income tax basic rate in 1979.
● Scrapping the reduced rate of income tax, 25 per cent on the first £750 of annual taxable income, in 1980.
● Making unemployment benefit taxable since July 1983.
● Forcing up rates by cutting Rate Support Grant to local authorities.

In the 1984 budget personal tax allowances were raised, but by 14 per cent less than the amount needed to remove the effect of tax increase since 1979.

Whatever happens to the overall tax burden, further big increases are likely in indirect taxation (see page 121).

Table 6   Tory tax handouts for the rich

Measures	Year of budget(s)	Annual cost (£m)[a]
Income Tax		
Concessions on higher rates/tax bands	1979, 1983	1,255
Investment income surcharge concessions	1979, 1983	355
abolition	1984	340
Other income tax concessions	various	45
Capital gains tax		
Indexation of post-1982 gains	1982	135
Various reliefs for trusts	1981, 1982	65
Other CGT concessions	various	105
Capital transfer tax		
Concessions on tax rates and thresholds	various	195
Other CTT concessions	1981–3	30
Stamp duty		
reduction on share transfers	1984	160
Total		**£2,685**

Note:

[a] Full-year revenue costs, updated to 1984–5 prices.

This was made clear by Treasury Minister of State Barney Heyhoe when he wrote to Geoffrey Howe (17 May 1984):

> The indirect tax base will have to be further extended. We have no set views at present about how it should be done, but it would be wrong to assume that any part of the tax system is immutable. VAT is a major tax on consumer spending and clearly has an important part to play.

Social security

Since 1979 the Tories have introduced six Social Security Acts. Each one has been designed to cut public spending (see Table 7).

Table 7

Year	Estimated savings (£m)
1980–1[a]	400
1981–2[a]	600
1982–3[a]	1,500
1983–4[a]	1,800
1984–5[b]	2,400
Total	**6,700**

Sources: [a] House of Commons Library;
[b] *Times*, 24 June 1984.

No claimants have been spared.

Pensioners

The link Labour had established between pension increases and the rise in prices or earnings (whichever was the higher) was broken in 1980. Since then, pensions have barely kept pace with prices. As a result, from November 1984, a married pensioner is £4.85 a week worse-off and a single pensioner £3. Pensioners have also been cheated in many other ways:

● In 1980, the government delayed the pension uprating by two weeks. It cost every married pensioner £12.30, but 'saved' the government £100 million. The government again delayed the November 1984 uprating by one week, at a cost to a married pensioner of £2.80 and a 'saving' to the Treasury of £60 million.
● In 1983, the government changed the way it calculated the rate of inflation for uprating pensions and benefits. Instead of basing the increase on the estimated annual rise in prices to

November, it was based on the actual rate of inflation to May. So in November 1983 benefits went up by just 3.7 per cent, when the rate of inflation in November was 4.8 per cent. The government 'saved' £500 million by this sleight-of-hand.

● Despite a pledge in their 1979 manifesto to 'phase out the "earnings rule"' during that parliament, the Tories froze the earning limit between 1980 and 1982. Although it subsequently increased to £70, the amount pensioners can earn before their pension is affected is still less in real terms than it was in 1979.

People with disabilities

■ *Our aim is to provide a coherent system of cash benefits to meet the costs of disability, so that more disabled people can support themselves and live normal lives.*

Conservative manifesto, 1979

Apart from a real improvement in mobility allowance, which helps less than 20 per cent of severely disabled people, the Tories' record on benefits for the disabled has been one of cuts and confusion.

Many benefits for disabled people – attendance allowance, invalidity benefit, non-contributory invalidity pension, industrial disablement benefit – have been reduced as a result of the Tories' breaking the link between long-term benefits and the movement in earnings.

In addition, invalidity benefit was cut by 5 per cent in November 1980 'in lieu of taxation'. The Tories have been unable to tax the benefit and the cut has remained. As a result of these two measures, a married invalidity pensioner is now £7.35 a week worse off. The government has promised to restore the 5 per cent cut in November 1985. But only half the invalidity pensioners will receive the full amount. For 150,000 of them, the increase in invalidity benefit will be offset by a reduction in their supplementary benefit. Another 150,000 will lose either the earnings-related or age-related addition to invalidity benefit when the cut is restored.

The government introduced a new benefit – Severe Disablement Allowance – in November 1984. It replaced non-contributory invalidity pension (NCIP) and the house-wives' non-contributory invalidity pension (HNCIP). While the notorious 'household duties' test has been done away with, another obstacle has been put in the way of claimants. All current NCIP and HNCIP recipients will be automatically transferred to the new benefit. But in future, people over 20 who become disabled without a contribution record and are unable to work will have to satisfy an 80 per cent disability test to qualify for benefit. It is estimated that 21,000 disabled people – mainly married women – who did not previously qualify for a benefit will now receive one, but at the expense of another 16,000 disabled people who will lose their rights to the benefit.

The unemployed
The unemployed have borne the brunt of the government's cuts in benefit. Expenditure on benefits for the jobless have almost trebled in real terms since 1979, as unemployment has risen relentlessly. But the incomes of those out of work have been savagely cut.

● In 1980 unemployment benefit was cut by 5 per cent 'in lieu of taxation'. Unemployment benefit was made taxable in July 1982, but the cut was not restored until November 1983.
● The earnings-related supplement was abolished in January 1982 – this would now be worth £18.70 a week to someone who had previously been receiving average earnings.
● Child additions to unemployment have been cut every year since 1980 and abolished altogether in November 1984.

The impact upon the incomes of the unemployed has been severe. Unemployment benefit is equivalent to just 18 per cent of average male manual earnings, compared to 32 per cent in 1979. Now, two-thirds of the unemployed have to turn to means-tested supplementary benefit for subsistence. Yet even here, they are discriminated against. Alone of all claimants under 60, they can never qualify for the long-term rate of benefit, worth an extra £11.55 a week to a married couple.

The sick

In April 1983 sickness benefit was abolished for the first eight weeks of illness, industrial injury benefit was abolished altogether. Instead, employers are now under a statutory duty to pay sick pay. But the rates laid down are the lowest relative to earnings of any EEC country and make no allowance for dependents. For those earning over £68 a week, the rate is £42.25. The low-paid are penalized in particular – they only qualify for a reduced level of pay: £35.45 for those earning between £50.50 and £68; and just £28.55 for those earning between £34 and £50.50.

When the Social Security Bill 1984 reaches the statute book, national insurance sickness benefit will be abolished altogether. Employers will have to pay statutory sick pay for up to 28 weeks.

Children

'**I attach a high priority to child benefit,**' declared Patrick Jenkin, then Secretary of State for Social Services in 1980. Such fine words have not been translated into action. Labour's proposed increase in child benefit in November 1979 was cancelled by the new Tory government, and child benefit was kept below its May 1979 value for the whole of the Tories' first administration. As a result, families were deprived of a total of £80.60 for each child over those four years. In November 1983, the cut was restored, and child benefit increased in line with inflation in November 1984 to £6.85. But it is worth little more now, in real terms, than Labour promised in November 1979. And in order to keep up with the increase in the married man's tax allowance, child benefit would need to be raised by 80p.

The children of families on national insurance benefits have been even harder hit. The Tories exploited some loose legislative drafting to cut child additions to unemployment and sickness benefit and invalidity and widows' pension in every year from 1980. Child additions for the unemployed and sick were cut from £1.70 in 1979 to just 15p in 1983. From November 1984, they have been abolished altogether. The child addition to invalidity benefit has been made subject to a means test.

● This year about 200,000 low-paid workers with children will have to wait up to a year to receive their rise in Family Income Supplement, thus losing out by as much as £100. In previous years, the new rate of family income supplement was paid automatically each November; but now families will have to wait until their annual award is due for renewal before receiving the higher rate. The government will 'save' £7 million by this little trick.

Supplementary benefit

The rise in unemployment, in particular the emergence of long-term unemployment, together with cuts in national insurance benefit, has led to an unprecedented increase in the number of people claiming means-tested supplementary benefit (see Table 8).

Table 8 Recipients of regular weekly payments of supplementary benefit

	Nov. 1979	Dec. 1982	Increase (%)
All supplementary benefit	2,855,000	4,254,000	49
All supplementary pensions	1,723,000	1,779,000	3.25
All supplementary allowance	1,132,000	2,475,000	118.6
Unemployed	566,000	1,717,000	203.4
NI widows over 60	19,000	16,000	[−15.8]
Other one-parent families	306,000	420,000	37.25
Sick and disabled	207,000	237,000	14.5
Others	32,000	85,000	165.6

● The numbers of children in families living on supplementary benefit almost doubled between December 1979 and 1982, from 923,000 to 1,721,000.
● The number of people dependent on supplementary benefit (claimants *and* their families) increased by almost 3 million between December 1979 and December 1983, from 4.4 million to 7.2 million.

But as the number of people on supplementary benefit rises, their standard of living has fallen.

- In 1980, the government reformed the legal basis of the scheme at 'no extra cost' – as a result, 0.5 million claimants made some gains in benefit, but over 1.75 million people lost out.
- The 1980 reforms restricted single payments to situations of extreme hardship. Families with children who had depended upon them for clothing were hit particularly hard. Between 1980 and 1981 the number of single payments for clothing fell by two-thirds.
- The families of strikers were punitively treated under the new rules. In assessing their entitlement to benefit, it is assumed they are receiving £16 a week strike pay, and their rights to claim other payments are severely restricted.
- From November 1984, 1.8 million claimants who receive heating or other weekly additions have had up to £1 deducted from their supplementary benefit as a result of the government modifying the 'available scale margin' rule.
- The standard of living afforded by supplementary benefit is meagre indeed. An unemployed man with a wife and two children under 11 receives just £64.75 a week plus his housing costs on which to live. All the needs of a young child have to met on £1.37 a day.

Supplementary benefit is inadequate even to meet the most simple needs, especially for families with children. A 1984 study by the Policy Studies Institute of families on supplementary benefit found that:

- a third of the children had no warm coat;
- over half the children had only one pair of shoes;
- half the families with children reported that they ran out of money most weeks before the next payment was due.

Housing benefits disaster

The Tories' housing benefit scheme which gives means-tested assistance with rent and rates to low-income households was fully introduced in April 1983. It replaced the previous dual system of supplementary benefit or rent and rate rebates and gave local authorities responsibility for the scheme. Housing benefit is now received by well over 7 million households – more than one household in three. The new scheme has been a financial and administrative disaster. It has led to:

• **A severe reduction in living standards for many households.** About 2.25 million households were made worse off with the introduction of the scheme because the government would commit no extra resources to it; 400,000 households lost their right to benefit altogether.

• **A more complex system, making it difficult to claim benefit.** There are still basically two different schemes, one for those on supplementary benefit (certificated cases) and another for those who are not (standard cases). A new benefit – housing benefit supplement – had to be introduced for those who would otherwise have lost their right to supplementary benefit. However, it is widely recognized that local authorities have experienced great difficulty in identifying those who are entitled to it.

• **Administrative chaos in many town halls and debt and despair for many tenants.** Local authorities had enormous difficulties in implementing the scheme, because of its complexity and the tight deadline set by government. Thousands of tenants have faced debt and eviction due to delays in receiving benefit.

• **A total failure of government policy.** The new scheme was designed to save civil service staff and money. But the Comptroller and Auditor General (November 1984) has found that the new scheme is more costly to operate than the range of benefits it replaced. Local authorities have had to take on more staff than the DHSS has shed. And in July 1984 the fourth report by the House of Commons Social Services Committee estimated that the new scheme will cost the tax-or ratepayer an additional £20 million a year.

Already the government has made cuts totalling £215 million a year in the scheme.

In April 1984:
• The taper (or the amount by which housing benefit is reduced as a claimant's income exceeds needs allowance) was

increased from 28p to 35p in the pound. Over 2 million households suffered some loss and 300,000 households lost benefit altogether as a result.

● Non-dependants over 18 living in the household were expected to make a greater contribution to housing costs.

In November 1984:
● The taper was further increased to 38p in the pound.
● The minimum amount of housing benefit payable was increased to 50p for both rent and rates (previously 20p for rent and 10p for rates) for those above the needs allowance.
● Non-dependent 16- and 17-year-olds not in receipt of supplementary benefit, Youth Training Scheme or severe disablement allowance were expected to contribute £3.30 a week towards the household's housing costs.

From April 1985:
● The special provisions to pay extra benefit in areas of high rent will be severely restricted. It is estimated that about half the local authorities will lose their high-rent status.

Crisis in the benefit offices
While the numbers claiming benefit rise inexorably, the government has cut the number of staff in benefit offices. The result is long delays in assessing and paying benefits, more mistakes in calculations and fewer home visits to elderly and disabled people.

● Between 1979 and 1983 the number of people claiming supplementary benefit rose from 3 million a week to over 4.6 million.
● Between 1979 and 1983 up to 10,000 jobs were cut from the DHSS and another 3,000 are due to go by 1988.
● In 1979 there was one member of staff to every 91 claimants; in 1983 there was one to every 131 claimants.

While the service to claimants has deteriorated, the government has greatly increased its anti-fraud activity. In

November 1984 it set up the so-called 'Specialist Claims Control' teams. They move from area to area working on the basis that claimants are guilty until proved innocent; they have been specifically instructed to 'dissuade' claimants suspected of fraud from claiming rather than become involved in the lengthy investigations needed for prosecution. The government claimed that up to January 1984 these teams had 'saved' £36 million in benefit. Research by the civil service unions casts considerable doubt on the validity of these figures.

But the government's anti-fraud activity stands in stark contrast to its concern to ensure that all those eligible for benefit claim their rights. Take-up rates for means-tested benefits, which the Tory government favours, are all extremely low.

● Only 71 per cent of those eligible claimed supplementary benefit in 1981.
● Only half the families entitled to family income supplement receive the benefit.
● The take-up rate in 1981 of rent rebates for families with children was 58 per cent; that for rate rebates was 45 per cent.

In 1981 alone, £900 million-worth of benefits went unclaimed.

Fowler benefit reviews
During 1983–4 Norman Fowler, Secretary of State for Health and Social Security, set up four major reviews into:

● benefits for children and young people;
● provision for retirement;
● supplementary benefits;
● housing benefit.

In addition, he instituted a survey of the extent of disability in Britain and set up an inter-departmental committee on maternity benefits. In his statement to the House of

Commons on 2 April 1984, the minister claimed that together these reviews constituted **'the most substantial examination of the social security system since the Beveridge Report 40 years ago'.** But the nature, operation and terms of reference of the reviews offer little hope for a comprehensive, radical and open debate on the future direction of social security:

● With the exception of the review into housing benefits, all are **under firm ministerial control** and packed with known government sympathizers.

● **The limited timetable** for the reviews gave organizations and individuals little time to offer considered submissions, nor did it allow for any research to be commissioned.

● **None of the evidence to the reviews has been published** by the government; and the reports of the reviews into supplementary benefit and benefits for children and young persons will not be published in advance of the government's own response to them.

● **The piecemeal nature of the reviews means that many important aspects of the social security system have been left out** and the relationships between different benefits ignored. For instance, the structure of the reviews did not allow for an examination of the inadequacies of the national insurance scheme which have given rise to the massive reliance on means-tested supplementary benefit.

● **The reviews are being carried out on an explicit 'nil cost' basis.** Any reforms to the system must be carried out within the present social security budget. Like previous 'nil cost' reforms in supplementary benefit and housing benefit, any improvements in benefit for some claimants will be at the expense of others.

● **The reviews specifically exclude an examination of tax reliefs and allowances** which are equally important in the redistribution of income. By limiting the reviews to the current social security budget, the government has seriously restricted the resources which could be 'channelled to where they are most needed'.

In fact, the reviews have little to do with identifying improvements that could be made in the welfare of pensioners, children, the unemployed and the poor. They are part of the government's overall strategy of cutting public expenditure in order to finance tax cuts. The social security budget now represents almost 30 per cent of total public expenditure. Major benefits are under threat as ministers look for savings.

Child benefit

Child benefit could be restricted to concentrate help on poorer families. This may sound superficially attractive but it is fundamentally flawed. Child benefit is now the only means of redistributing resources to families with children at all income levels. It represents society's commitment to the rearing of future generations. To restructure child benefit by means testing or taxing it would cause great problems.

● Unlike child benefit, whose take-up is almost 100 per cent, means-tested benefits are notoriously inefficient – they have low take-up, are expensive to administer and will add to the problems of the poverty trap for low-paid families.

● If child benefit were taxed at its present rate, this would mean a cut in benefit for many low-paid families who pay tax. In order to protect them, child benefit would have to be increased prior to taxation, but this would save little money since 96 per cent of taxpayers pay the standard rate of tax. Making child benefit taxable could also lead to demands to reintroduce child tax allowances which favour the better-off.

Pensions

The government is challenging the political consensus which was established with Labour's 1975 earnings-related pension scheme. The scheme will help break the link between poverty and old age when it achieves practical implementation in 1999. The Tories are raising unsubstantiated fears about the increasing burden of pensions. But:

● In the past 30 years, the number of pensioners has risen by 150 per cent and their share of total disposable income has doubled from 7 per cent in 1951 to 15 per cent in 1984–5. The 1975 scheme seeks to increase pensioners' share of disposable income by about 5 per cent over the next 40 years.

● As the government's own Social Security Advisory Committee has stated (second report, 1982–3), the developing contribution burden of providing a decent standard of living for pensioners 'is not greatly out of line with what is being paid already to meet the costs of exceptionally high unemployment. From 1983, employers and employees . . . have been paying contributions of 17.65 per cent to the National Insurance Fund. On the most costly of the Actuary's six central assumptions . . . the contribution to the Fund required to sustain the pension scheme would be 16.7 per cent of earnings by 2005–6 . . . Beyond that the contribution rate does become much higher . . . But at this distance in time we do not think there can be solid grounds for altering the scheme now for fear of all the worst outcomes occurring steadily for 40 years.'

Supplementary benefit

Supplementary benefit was designed as the 'safety net' of the social security system, but now it has become a major means of support for over 7 million people. The unprecedented scale of means-testing, the inadequacy of the scale rates – especially for families with children – and the low take-up rates, are major issues for supplementary benefit. However, they are not really addressed by the review. Instead, the government may try and introduce some of the proposals put forward in 1980 – for example, the introduction of a short-term flat rate level of benefit for new claimants, and a 'rationalization' of weekly additions and lump sums. The review into benefits for children and young people is also looking at 'the entitlement of 16-year-olds to supplementary benefit'.

Housing benefit

The review of housing benefit was set up amidst mounting criticism of the government's cuts in housing benefit. But the review's terms of reference make it clear that the government is still looking at ways to cut expenditure on housing benefits.

When setting it up, Norman Fowler said:

> The enormous growth of housing benefit expenditure and the income levels at which it is paid require further consideration.

But housing benefit expenditure has risen because of the massive increase in unemployment and the huge rise in council rents and rates resulting from government cuts in subsidies. The increase is *not* attributable to the generosity of the scheme. The government has specifically excluded the £3,500 million currently allocated to mortgage interest tax relief from the review.

4. Life in the 1980s

What the Tories have done to elderly people

Britain's 9.5 million pensioners have suffered a reduction in their living standards since 1979 as pensions have failed to keep up with earnings and vital community services have been cut back.

Pensions
The Tories broke the link between pension increases and the rise in average earnings, so denying pensioners a share in the general rise in living standards enjoyed by the working population. As a result, a married pensioner has lost £4.85 a week and a single pensioner £3 a week.

Services
The growing number of very elderly people in the population is placing extra pressures on the health and social services. But **the government has failed to provide the resources needed to maintain good-quality services for more people.** Patients are being discharged from hospital earlier, but local authorities have been prevented, through cuts in their Rate Support Grant, from providing the services they need in the community. The number of local authority meals-on-wheels, home helps and old people's homes has failed to keep up with the increase in the number of very elderly people. In some areas, old people have had to pay ever-increasing charges for these services. And as local authorities are unable to respond to all their needs, many old people are being forced into the private sector for the care and support they require.

Fuel poverty
Since May 1979 electricity prices have risen by 89 per cent

and gas prices by 130 per cent. Many elderly people are at risk from the cold. **On average, 48,000 more people over 60 die in the winter months than in the summer.**

Many elderly people are now forced to choose between eating and heating. But the Tories have scrapped Labour's Electricity Discount Scheme, which gave help to those on housing benefit as well as to those on supplementary benefit. Now, only pensioners receiving supplementary benefit can receive help with fuel bills. In November 1984, many of them lost up to £1 a week when the government offset part of their heating addition against their benefit.

Public transport
Fewer pensioners own cars than the rest of the population. For them, public transport is vital for getting about. **But the Tories have been busy undermining the ability of local authorities to provide good, cheap public transport.**

● The 1980 and 1982 Transport Acts enabled private operators to cream off the best routes, so jeopardizing the existence of less profitable, but no less essential, routes.
● Worse is to come in 1985. The abolition of the metropolitan counties and the total deregulation of public transport envisaged in the Tories' 1985 Transport Bill threatens whole networks of local bus services. Many more routes could disappear. There is no guarantee that concessionary fares for elderly people will remain.

What the Tories have done to families with children

Since 1979 children and their parents have been under attack by the self-styled 'Party of the Family'.

● **Throughout the whole of Thatcher's first adminstration, child benefit was kept below its May 1979 value.** Today, it is worth no more in real terms than Labour planned for November 1979. And it is 80p less than is needed to maintain parity with childless taxpayers.

● **Local authorities are no longer required to provide a meal of a certain nutritional standard for all their schoolchildren.** The government also scrapped the standard charge for school meals and the national scheme for free school dinners for children of low income families. Only children from families on supplementary benefit or family income supplement now qualify for free school meals. Some Tory local authorities have done away with school dinners except for those still entitled to free meals. Elsewhere, the standards of meals and the charges for them vary widely from authority to authority.

● Schools are suffering from the government's squeeze on local authority budgets. Successive reports by Her Majesty's Inspectorate pointed to falling standards, lack of equipment and an increase in parental contributions.

In Thatcher's Britain, child poverty has grown to alarming proportions.

● By 1981, one in four of Britain's children was living in or on the margins of poverty.
● Between December 1979 and 1982, the number of children living in families dependent on supplementary benefit almost doubled, to 1.75 million.
● The number of families caught in the poverty trap has trebled to 270,000 since 1979.
● 1.2 million children live in families where the head of the household is unemployed, 500,000 of them where unemployment has lasted over a year. Yet in November 1984, the government abolished child additions to unemployment benefit.

A study of families on supplementary benefit, by the Families Service Unit found:

● A third of the families never or only occasionally bought cheese, fresh meat, fresh fruit and vegetables.
● Four our of five of the families had to borrow money at times to make ends meet.

A recent study by researchers at the London School of Hygiene and Tropical Medicine has shown that long-term unemployment and its associated poverty can have serious consequences for the physical development of children. They found that by the age of two, children of long-term unemployed men could be an inch shorter than those of working parents, taking account of all the biological and social factors.

What the Tories have done to women

■ *I don't think that mothers have the same right to work as fathers. If the good Lord had intended us to have equal rights to go out to work, he wouldn't have created man and woman.*
Patrick Jenkin, Secretary of State for Social Services,
Man Alive, October 1979

Tories argue that married women – except for a privileged few like Margaret Thatcher – should stay at home to look after husband, children and elderly dependants. They should not enter paid employment.

Tory policies have been directed at reducing women's rights to decent jobs, decent pay and decent financial support. **Women are being forced out of paid jobs** back to their traditional role in the home through:

● **Cuts in community services**, pushing women out of their public sector jobs. Such cuts force women with family ties to fill the gap by giving up employment to look after the old, the young and the sick.
● **The 1980 Employment Act which seriously weakened women's right to paid maternity leave** and to protection from dismissal because of pregnancy.
● **The taxing of workplace nurseries**, which pushes up the cost of childcare for working women, making it even harder for them to continue in paid employment.

Even government statistics (which ignore non-claimants) admit to over a million unemployed women – more than

700,000 up on the May 1979 figures, an increase of 216 per cent. Since June 1983, female unemployment has risen dramatically – by 22 per cent. Yet still the Tories resist all attempts, such as Jo Richardson's Sex Equality Bill, to improve women's economic position.

Women tend to have jobs with lower pay and lower status than men because the Tories have:

● Removed protection from low-pay exploitation by the **abolition of the Fair Wages Resolution** (September 1983), the weakening of Wage Councils and the removal of Schedule 11 of the Employment Protection Act.

● Introduced deliberately complicated regulations to **amend the Equal Pay Act**. The Act was designed to incorporate equal pay for work of equal value and so bring Britain into line with the EEC directive on equal pay, which came into force in January 1984.

● **Cut spending on education and training**, thus limiting the ability of schools to develop girls' capacities to the full. In post-school education, the courses that most help women who have missed out on education are the first targets for economies.

Is it any wonder that women, who make up 40 per cent of the workforce, still make up 75 per cent of the low-paid? For every pound that a man earned in 1983, women earned only 75p – less than in 1977.

Women's access to financial support for themselves and dependents is being threatened by:

● **Cutting the real value of social security benefits** for pensioners, the unemployed and those receiving child benefit. Many of the people affected are women in need. Yet the Tories attack them yet further by insisting that mothers prove they can provide care for their children when at work before they can claim unemployment benefit.

● Introducing the **Matrimonial and Family Proceedings Act 1984**, which cut the right to maintenance of women and children after divorce. To encourage divorced wives to be

141

financially independent, the courts must take earnings into account and consider cutting off maintenance after a fixed period. The Act will also make the behaviour of partners during the marriage more relevant to the assessment of maintenance.

Women's fears of being physically attacked have increased. Sixty per cent of elderly women and nearly 40 per cent living in inner cities feel 'very unsafe' when walking alone at night, according to the British Crime Survey produced by the Home Office in 1983. Nearly 40 per cent of women aged 31 to 60 are affected. About one-third of all women – and over half of those living in inner cities – said they sometimes avoided going out at night because of their fears.

Such fears are not surprising given the Tory failure to reduce the ever-increasing levels of violent crime that have characterized their period in government. In 1983, the number of recorded offences of violence against the person exceeded 111,000 – over 16,000 more than in 1979.

So much for Thatcher's statement in July 1982 that 'the battle for women's rights has been largely won'.

What the Tories have done to ethnic minorities

Racial inequality

Racialism and racial discrimination continue to have a powerful impact on the lives of black people in Tory Britain. That is the view of the Policy Studies Institute survey, *Black and White Britain*, published in July 1984. The survey showed that the position of black British people is largely the same as it was when they first came to Britain in the 1950s and 1960s.

● **Black people are almost twice as likely to be unemployed as are white people** – and they tend to be unemployed for longer than whites.
● **Black workers tend to have jobs with lower pay and lower status than those of white workers**. Black men

generally earn about £20 a week less than white men.

● **Black children**, especially those of West Indian origin, **are not deriving the benefit that they should from** the **education** system. And few young blacks are being given places on employer-based Youth Training Schemes.

● **Black people live in dwellings inferior to the quality of British housing in general.** They are more often in smaller properties which, considering their larger household size, means more crowding. Asian households more often share amenities with other households.

● **Black people are more likely to face violence than whites.** According to *Black and White Britain*, racial violence and harassment is ten times worse than the level calculated by the 1981 Home Office study. The latter found that Afro-Caribbeans are 36 times and Asians 50 times more likely to be victims of violent attack than are white people.

● **Black men are two to three times more likely than white men to be stopped and searched by the police** – but few are arrested or charged, according to a 1983 Home Office study on police stop-and-search powers.

The Tories claim to support equal rights and equal opportunities for all British citizens, irrespective of race or religion. In practice, they have done nothing to eliminate racial discrimination, racial disadvantage or violence against black people.

Controlling the movement of black people
The Tories have consciously discriminated against black people. They have adopted tough policies on nationality and immigration – designed to keep blacks out and to appease the racists within their own ranks. Since 1979 there has also been an ominous shift to more clandestine, but no less discriminatory, internal controls.

Black people have been mostly relegated to second- and third-class British citizenship, with no right of entry to Britain, under the British Nationality Act 1981. First-class British citizenship which allows people to stay in Britain has gone to those, mainly white, people who were 'patrial' under the Tories' Immigration Act 1971. The rules are bent only for white immigrants like Zola Budd, who earned citizenship in record time in order to represent Britain in the Olympics.

Black families have been kept apart through the restrictive and racist 1980 and 1983 Immigration Rules. Only women who are British citizens can bring their husbands or fiancés to live with them – and then only if they satisfy immigration officials that they meet the necessary conditions. Children aged between 18 and 21 and elderly parents have to show that they are dependent, have no other relatives to turn to and have a standard of life substantially below the average in their own country before they are allowed to join their families in Britain. So much for the Tories' claim that they support family life!

Black visitors are refused entry – just because they are black. In 1983 a passenger from Ghana had a one in 30 chance of being refused entry to the UK as a visitor; one passenger in 76 was refused from Bangladesh. But only one in 7,800 visitors from Canada was refused.

Black people have increasingly been subjected to discriminatory internal controls. With the introduction of hospital charges for 'overseas visitors' in October 1982 and the exclusion of overstayers and alleged illegal entrants from claiming benefits under the Social Security Act 1980, black people have been frequently questioned about their eligibility for free NHS treatment and social security benefits. The aim is to force individuals out of the country before they can challenge Home Office decisions about their status.

In introducing the Commission for Racial Equality's annual report for 1983, its chair, Peter Newsam, challenged the government to take the lead in promoting equal opportunity and eliminating racial discrimination.

The government could do much to improve the position of black people – by taking action within the civil service to remove the disadvantage that black people still face, and by ensuring that government contractors operate equal employment policies. Instead, the government has given greater priority to measures to expand the voluntary repatriation scheme for immigrants. If you're black, the Tories' aim is to get rid of you – not to help you.

What the Tories have done to young people

■ *A nation which turns away from its young, dumps its own future as well as theirs . . . Yet Mrs Thatcher's government seems to treat youth like an illness which everyone must go through – like measles.*

Neil Kinnock, *Daily Mirror*, 23 January 1984

Young people who have been encouraged at school to have high aspirations find even their lowest expectations shattered on leaving. Many find themselves without a job, without good training and without prospects. Today's young people are becoming tomorrow's lost generation.

Few jobs
● Almost 1.28 million young people under 25 are registered unemployed. This does not include the 350,000 young people on the Youth Training Scheme and the thousands who are ineligible to claim benefit.
● Nearly 0.5 million school-leavers have not had a job since leaving school (June 1984).

Little training
The number of apprenticeships is down by a half since 1979. Many young people have been made redundant during their apprenticeships and have found themselves both without a job and training. Of course, some young people have been offered a place on the Youth Training Scheme, but they see it as little more than a low-paid alternative to work. Few who complete YTS in September will find a job by Christmas (pages 62–1). As Neil Kinnock has said: 'training without a real prospect of a job is like practising for a sport without ever playing a match.'

Loss of life and limb
This government does little to protect young people on YTS from industrial accidents. Since 1979, 27 young trainees have been killed; 10,000 have been injured – resulting in more than 100 amputations. The accident rate involving major injury

was 30 per cent higher among trainees than it was among workers in industry as a whole.

Wages versus jobs

This government believes that cutting young people's wages will lead to more jobs. Its position was summed up by Margaret Thatcher, speaking on BBC Radio 4 in January 1984: 'We would have more young people employed if somehow people who are responsible for negotiating wages had not insisted on much higher wages for young people.' Yet:

● Young workers' pay as a proportion of adults' is steadily dropping as youth unemployment continues to increase. Between April 1982 and 1983 young men's pay rose by less than 2 per cent compared with an average increase for adult males of over 8 per cent.

● The government's Young Workers Scheme aims to undercut their pay. The government has offered employers a £15-a-week bribe to keep young workers' weekly wages below £50. But the scheme is a flop. It offers no training at all. It has been expensive and wasteful. And it has created very few jobs.

Low incomes

● For those on YTS, the government has kept the training allowance down to a paltry £26.25 a week: it should have risen to £34 with inflation.

● For those lucky enough to get a place in higher education, grants are derisory. Those on further education courses get no compulsory grant.

● 16- and 17-year-olds who are without a job receive merely £17.30p a week supplementary benefit. If they refuse to enrol on a YTS course or don't complete it, they can have their benefit cut to £9.90 a week. Worse is likely to come. The cabinet minister reponsible for jobs, Lord Young, is proposing that young people should no longer receive supplementary benefit.

Despair and desperation

● One in four of unemployed people aged between 16 and

25 have contemplated suicide, according to a recent research study (Culham College Institute Study, September 1984).

Young people confronted by a no-hope future are increasingly attracted to an escapist route which is becoming cheap, fashionable and often deadly – drugs. There are 1,200 heroin addicts under 25 notified to the Home Office. But this is only the tip of the iceberg, since many other addicts are not known to officials and many others are hooked on other hard drugs. The government's response to this tragic social problem has been absurd.

Many young people want to leave home. But more and more find themselves homeless and helpless – forced to live in emergency night shelters, squalid bed-and-breakfasts and seedy bedsits – or worse, on the streets.

Increasing alienation

There is a crisis of confidence over the police force among young people. A recent survey, *Youth in the 80s*, found:

● Over two-thirds of young people mentioned involvement with the police as one of their worries or concerns and felt that police often mistakenly suspected them of wrongdoing. Half of young people of West Indian origin thought they were personally singled out.

The Police and Criminal Evidence Act will make matters worse. The 'reasonable suspicion' required to justify a stop-and-search is left to the individual police officer. Police have been known to use their stop-and-search powers on young people congregating in groups on the street, for example, or coming home late at night from parties – even for wearing unusual hair-styles. The Act will mark a return to 'sus' by the back door.

Discrimination against blacks

Young blacks, especially those of West Indian origin, are even more disadvantaged than white youths. They often live in depressed inner cities, leave school with few qualifications, without a job, and have little access to training. Black unemployment is double the level of white unemployment. Yet the Commission for Racial Equality has found 'virtually no black youngsters on most YTS schemes in multi-racial areas'.

Increased crime

As unemployment rises, so does crime. As William Whitelaw, then Shadow Home Secretary, stated in 1978:

> If boys and girls do not obtain jobs when they leave school, they feel that society has no need of them. If they feel that, they do not see any reason why they should take part in that society and comply with its rules.

The Tories' answer to this problem is not to create more jobs for young people. It is to force them into training schemes. Those who remain on the street and get into trouble with the police are given 'a short sharp shock' in detention centres, where the strict regime with drill and physical training may make the young offenders physically fit – but will do nothing to fit them for the outside world. The Prison Officers' Association has described the regime as 'demoralizing' and 'a waste of time'.

Research by the Home Office reveals that a staggering 84 per cent of 15–17-year-old males receiving custodial sentences are reconvicted within two years; yet the cost of keeping a young person locked up can be as high as £40,000 a year.

No voice and no power

The government believes that young people should be treated like children – seen but not heard, dependent not independent. The Thompson report on the youth service, *Experience and Participation*, called for increased youth participation, more social and political education, and improved facilities. The government has totally ignored these proposals. It has also refused to give statutory backing to the youth service.

The Tories want to churn out compliant and complacent

young people, while what society needs are independent and imaginative young people who can fully participate in and shape its future.

What the Tories have done to the unemployed

Life on the dole is one of unremitting hardship. As the number of unemployed has gone up, benefits have been cut. The number enduring unemployment for long periods is growing – by October 1984, 1.3 million had been out of work for more than a year.

Unemployment benefit is no longer the main source of income for the unemployed. Over two-thirds now suffer the indignity and stigma of claiming supplementary benefit. The standard of living provided is extremely low. An unemployed man with a wife and two children aged under 11 receives only £64.75 a week (plus housing costs) to live on. All the needs of a child have to be met on £1.37 a day.

This level of income is inadequate to meet the most basic needs. A recent study by the Policy Studies Institute showed that:

● Over half the families of unemployed men had children with second-hand shoes.
● Half the families with children reported a crisis most weeks in that they ran out of money before the week was up.

A further study by the Family Policies Study Centre in October 1984 showed that:

● One-third of the children had no warm coat.

The Tories have *deliberately* made life harder for the unemployed. They have reduced their living standards by:

● Cutting unemployment benefit by 5 per cent in 1980. The cut was not restored until November 1983.

- Abolishing the earnings-related supplement to unemployment benefits in January 1982. At that time it was worth £14 per week to the unemployed. Today an unemployed person, previously on average earnings, would be receiving an extra £18.70.
- Making unemployment benefit taxable from July 1983.
- Cutting child additions to unemployment benefit in every year since 1980, and finally abolishing them altogether in November 1984.

The human costs of unemployment are incalculable. Long-term unemployment is a debilitating disease. Severe hardship grinds people down. Many suffer from feelings of worthlessness, and from the isolation of being unable to afford to join in their usual social activities.

Recent studies on suicide have highlighted the harmful effects of unemployment on health and the stress and despair that it can bring:

- According to John Fox's study, *Unemployment and Mortality*, 1,800 men and 1,000 women could die this year because of the poverty and stress of being without work.
- Unemployed men are more than twice as likely to commit suicide as employed men.
- *Young and Unemployed*, by Dr L.J. Francis, found that one in four unemployed people aged between 16 and 25 has contemplated suicide.

What the Tories have done to disabled people

'The disabled cannot expect to be exempted from the sacrifices necessary for economic recovery.' Such was the bald statement of approach made by Reg Prentice, the Tories' first Minister for Social Security and the Disabled, when he addressed the Royal National Institute for the Blind, in July 1979.

There are at least 3.5 million disabled people in Britain,

of whom 1 million face considerable handicaps to their daily lives. Six years of Thatcher's government have dashed any hope they might have had of improvements in their living standards. Since 1979, economic and social hardships have been added to the handicaps they already face.

Living standards
Many benefits for disabled people – attendance allowance, industrial disablement benefit, invalidity benefit, invalid care allowance – which under Labour were increased in line with prices or earnings (whichever was the higher) are now protected only against inflation. So **the living standards of disabled people have fallen relative to those of the working population.**

In addition, 60,000 invalidity pensioners had their benefit cut by 5 per cent in November 1980. As a result, a married invalidity pensioner is now £7.35 a week worse-off than he would have been under Labour's policies. The Tories have said they will restore the cut in November 1985 – but only half of the country's invalidity pensioners will receive the whole amount. For the others, an increase in invalidity benefit will lead to a reduction in their other benefits.

Industrial injury benefit for those unable to work due to an industrial injury or disease was abolished in April 1983.

The Tories' reform of the supplementary benefits system in November 1980 hit disabled people hard. Previously about two-fifths of disabled claimants used to receive a single payment for exceptional needs in any one year. These grants are no longer available except in very limited circumstances.

Unemployed
Disabled people have suffered disproportionately from unemployment. They face an unemployment rate 50 per cent above the average and are three times as likely to be unemployed for more than a year. Yet the Manpower Services Commission has cut back on its services to disabled people – it has cut the number of disablement resettlement officers by 120 since 1979. The government has ignored requests for tougher action against employers who do not

fulfil their obligations to disabled people. Instead, it issued a voluntary code of practice on the employment of disabled people in November 1984.

Community services
Disabled people have also suffered from cuts in the health and social services which are equally important in maintaining their standard of living. **Aids and adaptations for disabled people were among the first things to be cut when the government started to squeeze local authority budgets.** Overall, spending on aids fell by 8 per cent in the first year of Thatcher's government. Local authorities have been reluctant to take up joint funding to enable them to finance a policy of care in the community because of uncertainty over their future financial position. There is less support for those disabled people living in the community, and the prospect of a life outside for those in hospital is receding rapidly.

Education
The Tories' 1981 Education Act was the government's 'main contribution' to the International Year of Disabled People. The Act implemented the recommendations of the Warnock Committee for integrating handicapped children into ordinary schools. But while the intentions were good, the government provided no new resources to make them a reality.

Discrimination
In November 1983 the government showed its true colours when it wheeled out its pay-roll vote to defeat Labour MP Bob Wareing's Private Member's Bill. The Bill would have outlawed discrimination against the disabled in areas such as employment and the use of services; it also proposed a Disablement Commission to investigate complaints. The Bill was based upon the recommendations of the Committee on Restrictions Against Disabled People, set up by the previous Labour government.

What the Tories have done to tenants

Under the Tories, tenants – public and private – have been neglected and exploited. Their housing costs have increased and their legal safeguards have been weakened, while housing conditions have been allowed to deteriorate.

And yet, on average, tenants are far poorer than home-owners. The 1982 *General Household Survey* shows that over two-thirds of households with a gross earned weekly income of £100 or less were council or private tenants; 61 per cent of families with no earners were tenants.

Council tenants
Housing cuts have bitten deep into the services for council tenants. Routine repairs and maintenance have been reduced leading to long-term decay. There are greater backlogs of repairs, allocations and enquiries.

Tenants face growing problems of structural defects, poor heating, asbestos, damp and insecurity. And yet it is precisely those least able to cope with these problems – pensioners, single parents, the unemployed – who are concentrated in council housing.

The 'right to buy' scheme has creamed off the best housing – 93 per cent of homes sold have been houses with gardens. But since no new homes are being built, tenants have less and less choice. The growing shortage makes transfers more difficult, and reduces the quality of offers.

Councils are forced to house tenants accepted as homeless in completely inappropriate accommodation. Three-quarters of households accepted as homeless in London are housed in bed-and-breakfast hotels, hostels or unimproved empty accommodation. For instance, by September 1984 housing shortage had forced Brent Council to place nearly 500 families in bed-and-breakfasts – at an annual cost of over £2.5 million.

Despite the appalling cuts in services, the Tories have forced councils to raise rents – from £6.40 in April 1979 to £14.70 in April 1984. More than 3.5 million out of the 5.5 million council tenants are now believed to be claiming housing benefit. But even housing benefit has been cut: in the most recent round of cuts (April 1984) *2 million* tenants lost benefit – some lost over £4 per week (for details on housing benefit, see page 130–1).

Private tenants

No one looked after private tenants in the change-over to housing benefit. In the administrative chaos, their benefit was often delayed, mislaid or miscalculated. Some tenants faced eviction threats long before their money arrived.

A study by the Social Policy Research Unit showed that only about 25 per cent of private tenants claim the benefit they are entitled to – and yet private tenants are among the poorest sections of the community.

Legal safeguards for private tenants have been eroded. Registered rents are now increased every two years instead of every three. Security of tenure has been reduced for some tenants and the government has turned a blind eye to Rent Act 'loopholes' (see page 67).

The worst conditions are found in 'houses in multiple occupation' (HMOs). As waiting lists lengthen, thousands of people are trapped in squalid, dangerous bedsits, bed-and-breakfast hotels, tenements, hostels and lodging houses – with no hope of decent homes.

● Nearly 300,000 households in England and Wales live in HMOs; 77 per cent live in HMOs that are sub-standard.
● The Institute of Environmental Health Officers says that four out of five HMOs need action to remedy defects.
● UK fire statistics show that between 1978–82 over 600 people were killed as a result of fire in HMOs. HMOs represent 1 per cent of Britain's housing stock, but account for one-third of all fire fatalities.

The government has repeatedly refused to bring in legislation to enforce minimum standards of fire precautions, repair or amenities.

What the Tories have done to inner cities

■ *A Conservative administration in the 1980s cannot avoid giving priority to inner-city policy. We are dealing with some of the poorest sections of our community, some of whom are living in conditions which are intolerable.*

Michael Heseltine, March 1983

The Tory approach to inner cities is entirely hypocritical. Inner-city areas have borne the brunt of public spending cuts. Yet they have:

● higher rates of unemployment;
● more people living in poor housing and longer waiting lists for council housing;
● higher proportions of elderly people living alone;
● higher proportions of children with special needs or children in care;
● higher rates of mental illness and handicap.

Service provision is *poorest* where need is *greatest* – especially in health and housing.

Inner cities face problems of dereliction and decay, high crime levels and vandalism. The frustration that led to the riots in 1981 has subsided into drug addiction and despair.

The government has deliberately and callously targeted deprived inner-city areas for the greatest cuts in local authority grant. For instance, Hackney is, according to the government's own figures, the most deprived area in the country: 28.6 per cent of the residents are unemployed; 32 per cent of families have single parents; 9 per cent live in overcrowded conditions; 11.9 per cent lack basic amenities. Yet this borough has lost £30 million in government grant over the past years. Now it has been rate-capped and told to cut £33 million to meet government targets.

Of the 18 authorities forced to cut services in 1985–6 by the government's rate-capping legislation – all but three cover high-stress, inner-city areas. Ten receive special funds from the Urban Programme set up by Labour to help inner city areas.

The Urban Programme itself has been cut by 15 per cent in real terms. The government was forced to backtrack this year on a proposed 50 per cent cut (spending was frozen at the 1983–4 level of £350 million), but Nigel Lawson is determined to make cuts of about £50 million this year.

'Partnership authorities' like Manchester, Birmingham, Newcastle and Lambeth were selected for funding under the Urban Programme because of their special need for additional grant-aid. Now they are subject to a grubby sleight-of-hand whereby money given through the programme is taken away in Rate Support Grant.

● Manchester got £4.5 million in extra 'Urban Programme' grant in 1984–5. But Manchester's RSG has been cut from £131 million in 1980–81 to £96 million in 1984–85 – a loss of £73 million in real terms.
● Lambeth got £3 million extra grant this year. But Lambeth's RSG has been cut from £60.6 million in 1980–81 to £37.3 million in 1984–5 – a loss of £41 million in real terms.

The government's response to the problems of the inner cities has been based on dogma. The Tory obsession with 'market' solutions means that plans and safeguards have been dismantled – merely hastening decay and dereliction. The Tories have:

● Repealed the Community Land Act, leaving local authorities without effective land purchase powers at the same time as taking powers to privatize land publicly held by local authorities, new towns and statutory bodies.
● Eroded the statutory town and county planning system, weakened public consultation and introduced charges for planning applications. Now they are proposing 'simplified planning zones' which would further erode local control over planning.
● Set up Urban Development Corporations in Merseyside and London's docklands which override the powers of democratically elected authorities.
● Set up 'Hongkong' style 'Enterprise Zones' – removing

planning and safety standards for residents and workers in a drive to attract 'sweat-shop' firms. Often, all that happens is that firms move from just outside the Enterprise Zone – disadvantaging neighbouring areas. A recent survey showed that 85 per cent of firms relocating into Enterprise Zones said they would have moved there anyway. (See pages 111–12.)

Government gimmicks – like the 'task force' in Liverpool – have failed to make any serious impact on unemployment or decline. Repeated appeals to the private sector to invest have failed.

Meanwhile, serious programmes to revive the inner city – local authority projects for jobs, homes and a better environment – have been starved of funds.

What the Tories have done to rural areas

No stone has been left unturned in the Tories' attack on Britain. Even the traditionally Tory rural shires have suffered – and suffered badly – under the Tory axe. Bus routes have been scrapped; village schools closed; public offices shut down; health services undermined. The whole fabric of life in the rural areas has been rent. And worse is yet to come.

Transport

In 1983–4 transport support was cut by a quarter. As a result, many villages will be cut off. In Norfolk, for instance:

- 72 villages are to lose their bus services;
- another 50 will lose their commuter services.

Recently, a Women's Institute survey showed that about half the rural population feared that their way of life would be drastically affected if cuts were made in existing bus services. A mere 4 per cent felt existing services fulfilled their transport needs.

And the spectre of Serpell – with its attack on rural rail routes – still hangs over the rural areas (see page 74). As do the Tories' recent proposals on bus licensing, which could spell the end for thousands of miles of 'unprofitable' rural bus routes.

Village schools
As a result of government cuts at all levels:

- 420 rural primary schools were closed between 1981 and 1983;
- a further 66 were approved for closure in the first six months of 1984.

Closing a village school is like tearing the heart out of the village, for a school is not just a centre for teaching the young. It is more a focal point for providing facilities for a wide range of social, recreational and educational activities. And LEAs have cut the provision of free transport down to the bone, bringing extra costs and worries to rural parents.

Village services
As a result of internal reviews, a number of government agencies have 'rationalized' their structures. Which in real terms means that villages and small market towns have lost DHSS offices, Job Centres and tax offices. Or they've had their opening hours reduced, making access that much more difficult.

Other services have been, or are about to be, withdrawn – usually as a consequence of the generally poor state of the economy. Barclays Bank has announced a 'reorganization' of its network – with the closure of 150 branches, many rural. And it's estimated that 50 per cent of the 12,000 villages with only a single shop could lose their shops in the next five years.

The viability of sub post offices is threatened by the tight financial limits imposed by the government and as a result of changes in the methods of benefit payments, while rural telephone charges are likely to rise and rural phone boxes disappear as a result of the privatization of British Telecom.

Housing
Rural housing has been hit a double blow. The rate of council

house sales in the rural areas has been far higher than the national average. At the same time, the building of rural houses, especially council houses, has slumped dramatically. Virtually all new building is by private developers, pushing up rural house prices and forcing low-paid villagers to seek cheaper accommodation in the towns.

Employment
Unemployment rates in many of Britain's rural areas remain way above the national average:

- in Cleveland, it's over 23 per cent;
- in the Western Isles, it's nearly 20 per cent.
- in Cornwall, over 19 per cent.
- in County Durham, over 18 per cent;
- in Shropshire over 16 per cent;

Despite this appalling record, the Development Commission, which is supposed to play a major role in promoting rural employment, has abandoned the Special Investment Areas and replaced them with Rural Development Areas. The latter cover 10 per cent less of the rural population. And the Development Commission budget for rural aid has been cut by nearly one-fifth, in real terms, since the Tories took office.

5. The right's attack on rights

Basic freedoms, which have long been taken for granted by the British people, are being denied by the Conservative government. The right of trade union members to organize effectively and to achieve their political objectives by supporting the Labour Party is being systematically eroded. The right even to join a union has been denied to workers at GCHQ. The police have prevented miners from moving around the country, and have been given increased powers which undermine the civil liberties of the individual. The right to know is being curtailed through the use of the Official Secrets Act, 'D' Notices and other measures.

In Thatcher's Britain, the Conservative Party has lost all claim to be the party of freedom. It is the Tories who are bringing the rule of law into question, by using the law to control the social tensions that their policies of mass unemployment have created.

Trade union rights

■ *There are people in this country who want to destroy the kind of free society we have . . . Many of these people are in the unions* [our emphasis].
> Margaret Thatcher, Thames TV, 24 April 1979

A central aim of the government has been to weaken and divide the trade unions. And, with the help of mass unemployment a battery of anti-union legislation, and a compliant judiciary, they have not been without success.

Thatcher finds it hard even to see why trade unions are needed. In her view, there is never *any* need for workers to act together to defend their jobs, rights, or pay: 'I do not believe that people who go on strike in this country have a legitimate cause.(*Hansard*, June 1982)

The loss of immunities

The judiciary, like the Tories, believes people have no need to go on strike. Under the ordinary common law – which it is the job of judges to interpret – trade unionism is simply not possible at all. For whenever workers combine together to take industrial action, they almost inevitably cause breaches of contract of one kind or another: they are, under common law, acting unlawfully – and can be threatened with injunctions and claims for damages. This is why, from the nineteenth century onwards, parliament has *had* to provide the unions with 'immunities'.

What the Tories have done – through no less than three different Acts of parliament – is to strip the unions of these 'immunities' over a wide range of *essential* trade union activities. And the unions are now liable for damages of up to £250,000 a time.

Under the Employment Acts of 1980 to 1982, there are new restrictions on the basic rights of trade unions to organize:

● **The right to strike.** By narrowing the definition of a 'trade dispute', the Tories have ruled out such essential forms of trade union activity as sympathy strikes and solidarity boycotts.

● **The right to reach agreement with employers on union membership.** Special ballots every five years, plus the need to obtain 80 per cent majorities, now make it difficult to make closed-shop agreements – thus undermining trade union strength. And workers who choose to ride on the backs of their colleagues by refusing to join a union can now claim compensation from the union if they lose their jobs.

● **The right to picket.** Workers can now no longer picket customers and suppliers of an employer in dispute. This means they have been deprived of the right to persuade other workers to help.

There are also restrictions on the rights of working people:

- **The rights of women at work.** Women can no longer claim the same jobs back after having children.
- **The right to 'fair wages'.** Employers can no longer be obliged to pay the 'going rate' for a particular trade; workers on public sector contracts have also lost *their* right to fair wages.

In addition, there are new provisions to make it easier to sack workers. The unfair dismissal laws have been weakened; employers can now give less notice of redundancies; it is now more difficult to prove unfair dismissal – especially in small firms; and the minimum compensation award of two weeks' pay has been abolished.

The Trade Union Act 1984

With the 1983 election out of the way, the Tories have now gone even further. The 1984 Act is designed to undermine the ability of unions to serve and protect their members. But it also aims to destroy the financial base of the Labour Party, the only political party able to defeat the Tories.

- **The Act imposes a rigid new balloting procedure for the election of top union officials.** In effect, this legislation allows the state to rewrite union rule-books, so taking away the right of workers to decide for themselves how their union should be organized. Indeed, backed by the powers of the High Court, the Act lays down detailed requirements – on how ballot papers should be distributed, collected and counted, on who can vote, on the need to maintain a register, and so on. The Act is a legal quagmire for the unions. It destroys their ability to match their procedures to their own diverse needs and circumstances. And it rules out indirect elections, even though these can often provide a far more representative outcome where there is a diversity of industries and trades.
- **Unions are now legally obliged to have a ballot before each and every call for industrial action.** If

action is taken without a ballot, the union must either disown it officially or risk having to meet massive claims for damaged – and face court injunctions. As the Tories well know, the Act will cripple the ability of unions to respond quickly, flexibly and effectively, or to mobilize support among their members. It will tip the balance of advantage at work decisively in favour of the employers – and especially of *bad* employers. It will divide the unions, both among themselves and from their members (as was seen in the Austin Rover dispute, in November 1984). By tying the hands of negotiators, it is likely to harden attitudes, prolong disputes and undermine good industrial relations.

● **Unions must now ballot their members every ten years on whether or not to have political funds.** The Act represents a deliberate attempt to stop unions from involving themselves in any kind of political action – from meetings or campaigning to save jobs, right through to giving support, financial or otherwise, to the Labour Party. Under the Act, *only* if there is a political fund can a union finance such activities. Such political funds cannot be topped up from the general funds of the union. And if there is *any* breach of the detailed requirements laid down by the Act, the union will be open to damages and injunctions from the courts.

It is this last part of the Act which exposes most clearly the Tory aim: it will provide regular and disruptive divisions within unions over the principle of maintaining political funds; and it will prevent unions from properly defending the interests of their members by *all* the means open to them – means which have to include campaigns, meetings and lobbies of parliament.

The Act is an attempt to destroy the only effective political opposition to the Tories: the Labour Party. There is nothing whatever in the Act to ensure that companies – which, of course, provide a major share of Tory income – ballot *their* shareholders and employees before making donations to political parties. The unions, on the other hand, are bound hand and foot. Indeed, even if a union does have a substantial minority of members who want to co-operate in helping to fund the Labour Party, it will be allowed to do nothing whatever to help collect contributions or assist the party.

GCHQ

On Wednesday 25 January 1984, the Foreign Secretary, Sir Geoffrey Howe, announced in the House of Commons that all civil servants working at the government communications headquarters, GCHQ, were to be deprived of their trade union rights. Union leaders were given just ten minutes' notice of the announcement.

With immediate effect, GCHQ staff were deprived of all their rights under employment protection legislation, including the right to appeal to an industrial tribunal against unfair dismissal. Staff were also told that their right to belong to a trade union would be withdrawn from 1 March 1984. Those who agreed to sign an official form surrendering their rights were to be paid £1,000. Those who refused to sign were threatened with dismissal.

The government ban was the clearest possible violation of the freedom of individual workers to associate in trade unions. It flew in the face of a series of international labour and human rights conventions. However, the government's case for the ban never went beyond the innovation of sweeping 'national security' reasons, together with references to past industrial action at GCHQ between 1979 and 1981.

The government has never satisfactorily explained the extraordinary delay between the 1981 industrial action and the ban itself nearly three years later. Nor has it succeeded in proving a single case where industrial action at GCHQ had actually engendered national security.

The government ban was condemned by all the opposition parties in parliament, virtually all the national press, senior civil servants in the Cabinet Office, a recent former head of the civil service, the TUC, all the civil service trade unions and, according to the opinion polls, a large majority of public opinion.

● Among the most damning critics of the government was the

164

all-party Commons Select Committee on Employment. Despite a 6:5 Conservative majority on the committee, and despite a government order preventing trade union witnesses from GCHQ appearing before it, the committee's final report demolished the government's arguments for the ban and called unanimously for a reversal of the decision.

● The International Labour Organization ruled in June 1984 that the ban is a breach of the convention governing freedom of association. In July the High Court ruled that the government's action was invalid, with Justice Glidewell declaring that the government's failure to consult staff and unions at GCHQ was a breach of natural justice. However, in August the Court of Appeal overturned this decision, ruling that the courts had no power to interfere with government decisions taken in the interests of 'national security'. The unions appealed to the House of Lords, which upheld the decision of the Court of Appeal.

Despite the government's action, at least 100 GCHQ staff have resisted intimidation and have courageously maintained their trade union membership throughout; the unions say they now have 300 members there. At the same time, there have been persistent reports of low morale among the staff generally at GCHQ as result of the government's behaviour. The government plans to set up its own staff association but it has been reported that only a minority of GCHQ staff have voted to support it.

One probable reason for the ban is connected with the government's intention to introduce 'lie detector' machines for GCHQ staff. The unions and GCHQ staff have made clear their opposition to these machines, whose reliability has been widely questioned. Clearly, the government hopes that by removing union protection it will be easier to impose them on reluctant staff.

The right to know

The Tories pay much lip-service to 'freedom'. But they have no intention of opening up government so that people can see how and why decisions are taken in their name. On the contrary, the Thatcher period has been marked by further restrictions on the public's right to know.

● In its first year the government introduced a Protection of Information Bill, described in the *Daily Mail* (2 November 1979) as 'honestly and unashamedly devoted to the belief that government is a secret process and that press and public should be told only what Whitehall considers good for them'. But the Bill was so widely criticized, even by Tory sympathizers, that the government was forced to withdraw it. Nevertheless, the government remains committed to the thinking behind the abortive Bill.

● Senior civil servants have been prevented from even speaking to the all-party 1984 Campaign for Freedom of Information.

● The government is actively using the notorious Section 2 of the Official Secrets Act to clamp down on embarrassing leaks. This Section – which makes the disclosure of almost any official information a criminal offence – was once described by the present Home Secretary as 'indefensible'.

The Tisdall case
The most notorious instance of the Tory clamp-down is the Tisdall case. In October 1983 the *Guardian* published a leaked memorandum from Defence Secretary Michael Heseltine. The newspaper was taken to court and ordered to hand over the document so that it could be traced. Following this, a 23-year-old junior civil servant, Sarah Tisdall, was prosecuted under Section 2 of the Official Secrets Act. She pleaded guilty and was sentenced to six months' imprisonment in March 1984.

The published document was concerned with Heseltine's plans to manage the news of the arrival of cruise missiles. It detailed nothing more than a public relations stunt. Although the prosecuting counsel acknowledged that there had been no damage to national security, the judge ruled that 'in these days' an example had to be made. The Appeal Court upheld the sentence, with the Lord Chief Justice saying that it would be impossible to run a government 'if confidential and secret memoranda are being divulged to outsiders by members of staff.'

A concerted clamp-down
It is clear that the Tory government is determined to wield the big stick to make sure we are kept in the dark. The *Sunday Times* (23 September 1984) reported a former Thatcher minister as saying: 'The order has gone out from on high that, if there is a leak, you must call the police.' There is plenty of evidence to bear this out:

● Clive Ponting, a Ministry of Defence official, was charged under the Official Secrets Act with supplying documents relating to the sinking of the *Belgrano*, including one which demonstrated the government's desire to withhold information from a Commons Select Committee.

● Since 1984, police raids in the hunt for the source of leaks have become commonplace. The offices of Friends of the Earth, Greenpeace and the *New Statesman* have all been visited. When journalist Duncan Campbell was involved in a cycling accident, the police took away his papers and went on a 'fishing expedition' at his home; they found nothing incriminating.

Despite their apparent concern with leaks, Tory ministers regularly leak proposals when it suits them. In Thatcher's Britain, it seems, the public is entitled to know only what the government thinks it should be told.

Personal files
There has been growing concern about the vast range of information kept on individual citizens in personal files, and the failure of the law to control the collection and use of such information.

The last Labour government set up a committee which recommended action as long ago as 1978. For four years the Tory government did nothing. It was only when faced with the need to satisfy a Council of Europe convention that the

Tories reluctantly introduced legislation to control data-banks and to grant limited individual access to personal files. This Bill (which fell because of the general election) and its successor represented the minimum the government thought it could get away with in order to satisfy the convention. As William Whitelaw, then Home Secretary, stated: 'We must ensure that the information technology industry flourishes, and that is the purpose of this Bill.'

What is now the Data Protection Act was improved during its passage through parliament; but it is still inadequate. It covers only computer-held data, not manual records, and even for computerized records there are many very wide-ranging exemptions. Also, it will take at least two years for the provisions to come into effect.

The Tory government also opposed the inclusion of statutory controls on telephone-tapping in the Telecommunications Bill. Only after being defeated on this point in the House of Lords in February 1984 did the government reluctantly agree to bring in new legislation.

The Police

The Police Act
■ *For the first time we have seen the police having to resort to some kind of paramilitary style of policing, which we have always associated with continental police forces and always prided ourselves on having avoided having to introduce.*

John Alderson, former Chief Constable of Devon and Cornwall, *Diverse Reports*, 17 October 1984

Central to the goverment's strategy is the Police and Criminal Evidence Act. The previous, much criticized Police Bill, which fell at the last general election, was reintroduced in amended form. Some of the worst features of the Bill have been removed. But it will still dramatically increase police powers and legitimize current abuses. The Act will:

● Allow the police to get a warrant to search the house or

workplace of someone not even suspected of an offence.

● Greatly increase police powers to stop and search people in the street and set up roadblocks.

● Allow the police to detain someone suspected of a 'serious offence' in police custody without charge for four days – six if over a weekend – with no right to see a solicitor for 36 hours.

● Create a new power of arrest for any offence, even the most minor, like dropping litter.

● Authorize intimate body searches for articles which could cause physical injury, strip searches and the taking of fingerprints – whether or not the suspect consents.

Rather than jeopardize the Act's passage, the government also reluctantly accepted a Lords amendment which makes racially discriminatory action by the police an offence under the Police Disciplinary Code. The amendment was passed with Labour support, with 29 Conservative MPs against. However, the Act still fails to:

● Provide adequate protection for suspects in police custody. There is no means of effective enforcement of the Codes of Practice (which will replace the Judges' Rules). Breach of the new rules – for example, in respect of treatment of young and mentally handicapped suspects – will not automatically make the evidence so obtained inadmissible in court.

● Introduce a truly independent police complaints procedure. Investigation of all complaints will still be left in the hands of the police, thereby perpetuating a system in which the public has no confidence.

● Improve police accountability to the community. The proposed public consultation is one-way only. There will be no obligation on the police even to take part, let alone provide any information or take the public's views into account. Nor will any provision be made for increasing the accountability of the police to the public or its elected representatives.

Exercise of these powers will mean that innocent people – as well as criminals – will be vulnerable to infringements of their liberty and abuse of their rights.

Policing the miners' strike

It is particularly disturbing that some of the new powers proposed under the Police Act were used by the police against striking miners and their families even before the Bill became law.

The massive police operation against the miners has taken many forms:

● **Freedom of movement has been interfered with** by the creation of roadblocks, involving a huge extension of common law powers. The declared aim of the police has been to prevent an unspecified breach of the peace, at some unknown time, at some unknown place. And it has affected not only pickets; other people have been prevented from going to court, calling at their union HQ, visiting their relatives, or even returning to their homes. The alternative has been the threat of arrest for 'obstruction'.

● **The police have actively attempted to help the National Coal Board by preventing picketing:** pickets on picket lines have been arrested for infringement of ancient laws ('watching and besetting') or for cries of 'scab' (insulting language); rather than pursue charges to conviction, the police have used bail conditions to deter picketing. Three-quarters of all the charges have involved obstructions; only a one-tenth have been connected with violence and assault.

● **People collecting money and food for the miners have been harassed and arrested.** Collections have been confiscated. Food deliveries have been hindered.

● **Police anti-riot tactics have intensified violence.** The decision to keep the gates of the mines open 'at all costs' – taken as much by the government as by police officers – has exacerbated the situation.

The major responsibility for these disturbing developments lies with the government. It has sanctioned police tactics on the picket lines and the increasing national control of the police through the unaccountable National Recording Centre. The government is using the police not to defend the law, but as a means of implementing Tory policy – be it on pit closures, eroding trade union rights or the right to demonstrate at places like Greenham Common.

Policing by coercion rather than by consent will create an ever greater divide between the police and the public. It will not help the fight against crime. To be effective in fighting crime, the police *must* have the confidence of the whole community. But they are losing that support – not only by appearing to take sides in this dispute, but also through the growing spectre of a national police force and the lack of accountability of the police to the local communities they are employed to serve.

As well as being forced to meet many of the costs of the police operation, police throughout the country are seriously affected by the removal of many police officers from duties in their areas to police the picket lines. Senior police officers have already expressed concern about the increased crime and lower detection rates, resulting from fewer police officers on the streets. But there is very little that local people can do about it. Though proper accountability is in the common interest of communities *and* the police, the government refuses to give local people a real say in the determination of police policy within their areas.

More and more hardware
Another disturbing development is the dramatic increase in the weaponry at the disposal of our supposedly unarmed police. Since the urban riots of 1981, plastic bullets, CS gas and water cannon have been made available to the police in a number of areas. Guns were issued for over 14,000 operations against persons known or believed to be armed in London alone, in 1983. In spite of the increasing public concern about the use of guns by the police following the shooting of Stephen Waldorf, the Home Secretary allowed the London police to be issued with 9mm sub-machine guns. Such weapons are incompatible with civil policing.

Northern Ireland

The economy
Tory policies have turned Northern Ireland into an economic and industrial wasteland. Right across the province, factories have closed and unemployment has soared. In May 1979, the number of unemployed was 60,814 (10.7 per cent of the population). By September 1984 it had reached a record level of 127,089 (21.9 per cent). The latest (January 1985) figures show that there are still 123,105 people unemployed (21.3 per cent). A number of alarming facts highlight the seriousness of the problem:

● Over half the unemployed have been out of work for over a year;
● Manufacturing employment has fallen by 27 per cent since May 1979;
● The level of unemployment has not been below 20 per cent since May 1982;
● Industrial output has dropped 12 per cent since May 1979.

Since May 1979, factory closures and job losses have included:

● Courtaulds polyester, fibres: 3,800 jobs
● De Lorean cars: 2,600 jobs
● Harland and Wolff shipyard: 2,500 jobs
● Michelin tyres: 2,250 jobs
● ICI polyester: 1,100 jobs
● Grundig electrics: 1,100 jobs
● British Enkalon fibres: 800 jobs

The political front
On the political front the attempt to set up a representative Northern Ireland Assembly has proved to be a failure. Both the SDLP and Sinn Fein, who won seats to the Assembly in the October 1982 elections, have refused to take part. The Assembly has no powers to do anything constructive for the people of Northern Ireland; nor are there any plans to give it

any real powers. With the resignation in September 1984 of James Prior, its main proponent, the Assembly is not likely to have much of a future.

The publication of the report of the New Ireland Forum in May 1984 received a hostile response from the Tories. The report outlined three forms of political structures – unitary state, federal/confederal, and joint authority – to be considered as a basis for discussions on the future of Ireland, North and South. Last November, Margaret Thatcher ruled out all three options. In the only parliamentary debate held to discuss the report in July 1984, James Prior indicated that the Tories might consider ways of improving political, social, and economic co-operation. To date very little progress has been made in this area.

The security problem

Added to economic and political misery is the Tories hard line attitude to the security problem. Their harsh methods have resulted in:

- More plastic bullets (29,601) fired in 1981 than the total of all other years since 1973;
- Ten deaths (four of them children of 15 years and under) by plastic bullets in the last five years;
- The deaths of ten hunger strikers in 1981;
- More people (1,174) detained in 1983 under the Prevention of Terrorism Act in Northern Ireland than in the first six years of the Act's existence. Less than 1 per cent of those detained in Northern Ireland have been charged.
- An excessive number of strip searches in Armagh's female prison. There have been almost 2,000 strip searches since their introduction in November 1982.
- Widespread accusations of a 'shoot to kill' policy on the part of the security forces;
- Large numbers of people arrested, detained and, often, convicted in the no-jury courts on the uncorroborated evidence of 'supergrasses'.

In March 1984, the Tories introduced a new Prevention

of Terrorism Act to replace the 1976 Act. Like the 1976 Act, it applies throughout the UK. The Labour Party voted against the new Act, and is firmly committed to its repeal. Labour will also end the use of plastic bullets in Northern Ireland.

The legal system

There is also deep concern in Northern Ireland about the legal system. The system was strongly criticized in the 1984 Annual Report of the government-appointed Standing Advisory Commission on Human Rights. There was a review for the government of the emergency legislation undertaken by Sir George Baker, but the report, published in 1984, proposed no major reform; it was largely uncritical of the system. Labour is committed to a major reassessment of the whole issue.

6. Energy and the environment

The coal dispute

The miners' strike – to save jobs, pits and communities – was deliberately engineered by the Tory government. In March 1984, the Coal Board proposed to reduce deep-mined production by 4 million tonnes, to close 20 pits, and to lose 20,000 jobs . . . all over just 12 months.

The proposal can be traced back to the Tories' Coal Industry Acts of 1980 and 1982. These Acts indicated that all grants to the industry would be phased out by March 1988. After that date, the industry would be expected to break even. And the January 1985 White Paper on Public Expenditure confirms this.

Yet the only way in which the industry could break even by 1988 – as the Tories knew – would be to close dozens of so-called 'uneconomic' pits. The Tory proposal meant:

- a **reduction** in deep-mined production in 1984/5 from 101.4m tonnes to 97.4m tonnes;
- the **closure** of 20 pits with the loss of 20,000 jobs over 12 months;
- the **closure** of a further 50 pits with the loss of 50,000 jobs over eight years.

The Tory attack on the miners has been an integral part of their attack on the rights won by the trade union movement over the years.

Even before they took office, the Tories were planning to do battle with the trade unions, particularly those in the public sector. A Tory policy group document (the 'Ridley Plan') was drawn up by Nicholas Ridley MP, on the nationalized industries. As it made clear, the methods used to make these industries profitable 'might mean that men would be laid off or uneconomic plants would be closed down, or whole businesses sold off or liquidated'. (*Economist*, 27 May 1978).

In 1980, the Tories appointed Ian MacGregor as chairman of the British Steel Corporation. While he was at British Steel the number of employees was more than halved.

In 1983, MacGregor was appointed as chairman of the National Coal Board. The message to the miners was clear: the Tories, through MacGregor, were determined to destroy a large proportion of the coal industry. In 1981, the Tories had not been ready to take on the miners: they retreated under threat of a massive strike over pit closures. By 1984, they were fully prepared. The 'Ridley Plan' determined their tactics, which were to:

● Build up maximum coal stocks, particularly at the power stations.
● Make contingency plans for the import of coal.
● Encourage the recruitment of non-union lorry drivers by haulage companies to help remove coal where necessary.
● Introduce dual coal and oil firing in all power stations, as quickly as possible.

From the start the Tory attack on the striking miners took on an aggressive, war-like tone. In a speech to the right-wing 1922 Committee on 19 July 1984, Margaret Thatcher said:

In the Falklands we had to fight the enemy without.
Here the enemy is within and it is much more difficult
to fight, but just as dangerous to liberty.

But who is it that is a danger to liberty? It is not the miners. If any group can be accused of endangering liberty it is the Tories. Back in 1978, the 'Ridley Plan' laid down the line:

There should be a large mobile squad of police equipped
and prepared to uphold the laws against violent
picketing.

The police, in effect, have been used to defeat the strike. 'Policing the Miners' Strike' on pages 168–71 sets out the details. Police activities include:

● Deliberate interference with ordinary people's freedom of movement;
● The use of police anti-riot tactics which have intensified violence;
● The harassment and arrest of people collecting money and food for the miners.

But the government has also manipulated the social security system, in the dispute, to try to *starve* the miners back to work. This they have done by:

● stopping £16 per week of benefit on the pretence that the miners are receiving this amount of strike pay;
● denying miners' wives their entitlement to FIS (Family Income Supplement), on the totally false premise that the families' incomes in this strike remain at the level before the overtime ban;
● denying discretionary maternity benefits for mothers;
● delaying the payment of supplementary benefits;
● making deductions from benefit because families have received gifts of food and other essentials.

The cost of pit closures
The aim of the Tories and the NCB is to eliminate the 10–12 per cent of capacity which accounts for over £300 million in so-called lost revenue. Yet this book-keeping ignores entirely the costs to the community of closing the pits:

● **Social devastation for whole communities.** As the coal fields lie in areas of high unemployment, there is little or no chance of alternative work for miners who are made redundant. Pit closures will mean families lose their livelihood, and the decay of whole communities.
● **Thousands of millions of pounds in cost to the nation,**

in terms of redundancy payments and social security benefits for redundant miners, in lost tax revenues, and in extra rent and rate rebates. These sums will dwarf any so-called savings. The NCB say that, over ten years, they could save £2.4 billion. But as the NUM has shown, the cost to public funds could be as much as £5.5 billion.

The pace of closures

The Tories plan to end grant support to the industry by 1988, and to concentrate investment on new low-cost pits, such as in the Vale of Belvoir and at Selby. This will inevitably mean that the highest cost pits have to close over a very short period of time.

Already under the Tories, pits have been closing at **twice the rate** of those under the last Labour government. And redundancies have proceeded at **more than twice the rate** of those under Labour.

Table 9. Number of Collieries and Average Manpower 1974–1984

Year ending March	Number of collieries	Average manpower
1974	259	252,000
1975	246	246,000
1976	241	247,000
1977	238	242,000
1978	231	240,500
1979	223	234,900
1980	219	232,500
1981	211	229,800
1982	200	218,500
1983	191	207,600
1984	170	191,500

Source: NCB Annual Reports and Accounts.

But it is not only pits that have been closing at an

alarming rate. There are 42 power stations (mostly coal-fired) which have also been closed. At the end of March 1984, the CEGB was operating 90 power stations with a declared net capability of 51,028 MW – nearly 4,000 MW less than on the previous year.

Costs of the strike
According to the Tories, it is well worth bearing the costs of the strike. In the House of Commons on 31 July 1984, Nigel Lawson said: 'Even in narrow financial terms, it represents a worthwhile investment for the nation.'

Yet the cost, in terms of extra public spending and lost revenue, was estimated by Simon and Coates for *Weekend World* (24 January 1985) to be well over £2,000 million. Of this, nearly £200 million is accounted for by extra police costs alone; £720 million in extra costs for the electricity industry; and nearly £1,000 million in extra outlay for the NCB. **The weekly cost reached over £80 million by November 1984**.

It has also cost the economy as a whole, some £5,000 million in all, more than 2 per cent of our national output.

A deliberate act
The miners' strike, contrary to Tory propaganda, was not the result of a spontaneous decision by the miners at Cortonwood colliery, one of the five pits designated for short-term closure. It was carefully engineered by the Tories to break the strength of the miners' union and **to destroy mining jobs and the mining communities in the process**.

Energy

Nuclear power
Within six months of taking office in May 1979, the Tories announced a major extension to Britain's nuclear programme. On 18 December David Howell, then Secretary of State for Energy, told the House of Commons:

the electricity supply industry has advised that even on cautious assumptions it would need to order at least one new nuclear power station a year in the decade from 1982 or a programme of the order of 15,000 mw over ten years. We consider this is a reasonable prospect against which the nuclear and power plant industries can plan.

The choice of reactor for the new programme is the American Pressurized Water Reactor (PWR), although with British modifications. A public inquiry into a CEGB planning application to build the first PWR at Sizewell, Suffolk, has been sitting since January 1983. The Sizewell PWR is expected to cost in the region of £1.15 billion at March 1982 prices.

Since the original announcement in December 1979, the CEGB has indicated that it now wishes to build about five or six PWRs. But even such a reduced programme will substantially increase nuclear power's contribution and cost at least £5.5 billion to £7 billion.

At present, nuclear power provides about 16 per cent of Britain's electricity. When the British-based Advanced Gas Cooled Reactor programme is completed in 1986, this will increase to 20 per cent or more. An extra five or six PWRs will further increase nuclear power's contribution. The size of the increase will depend upon the rate at which the 30-year-old Magnox nuclear reactors are phased out.

Not content with this, however, the Tories would like a further increase. At the moment, the 16 per cent of electricity generated by nuclear power is equivalent to 18 million tonnes of coal (million tonnes of coal equivalent: mtce). Whitehall figures, however, revealed in the *Guardian* (28 November 1984), show that this could increase to between 38 and 73 mtce by the year 2000 and, between 69 and 155 mtce by 2010.

This increased contribution from nuclear power will not be in *addition* to that presently made by coal. It is very unlikely that energy demand will have increased by either 73 or 155 mtce by the year 2000 or 2010. With improvements in energy efficiency and, hopefully, greater conservation of energy, demand will rise at a much slower rate than in previous years.

One thing is clear, therefore: the Tories are intent on scaling down the contribution the coal industry makes to electricity generation. Over the past five years the industry has provided a yearly average of 75 million tonnes of coal to the CEGB. The CEGB is easily the coal industry's biggest customer. Accordingly, any extension of nuclear power can only be achieved at the expense of coal.

Renewable sources

In contrast to its support for nuclear power, the government has been less than enthusiastic about developing alternative or renewable sources of energy. In 1984–5 the Tories expect to spend about £14 million on reseach and development into renewable sources, compared with £56 million which the Atomic Energy Authority spent in 1983–4 on the Dounreay Fast Breeder Reactor *alone*.

Conservation

Energy conservation also receives little encouragement from the Tories. The Energy Efficiency Office was set up in October 1983 to encourage a more efficient use of energy; but the Homes Insulation Scheme, an important means of cutting household costs and saving energy, has been allocated a mere £35 million in the financial year 1984–5.

The environment

Britain's natural environment is under threat. The health of the people is in danger. Acid rain is destroying the countryside; leaded petrol is harming children; industrial waste is polluting our rivers; nuclear waste is threatening our future. The Tories respond with complacent platitudes and ineffectual gestures. But what is needed is swift, decisive action.

Acid rain

Acid rain produced in Britain's power stations is destroying our countryside and our buildings – and those of other countries. But the Tory government refuses to do anything.

- Britain is responsible for around 10 per cent of all the acid rain produced in Europe – about 40 million tonnes a year.
- About one-third of the acid rain produced in Britain is deposited here. Another third falls in the sea. But the rest is 'exported' – mainly to Scandinavia.
- More sulphur dioxide and nitrogen oxides – which cause acid rain – is discharged into the atmosphere in Britain than in any other country in the rest of Western Europe.

Most of the reductions have been made by industry. But the major emitter is the Central Electricity Generating Board (CEGB), which has made *no* significant reductions. Proposals for 'cleaning' flue emissions of sulphur dioxide have been rejected by the CEGB and the government as 'too costly'.

- Even on CEGB figures the total cost of desulphurization would only add 6 per cent to electricity prices over ten years. Yet between 1979 and 1984 domestic electricity prices were increased by nearly 90 per cent.
- The government has chosen to spend vast sums on developing nuclear power rather than investing in new combustion technology which would reduce pollution and increase energy efficiency.

The Tory government has led an increasingly isolated campaign against any British commitment to cut back on acid rain. As the Tories' own Bow Group put it, the government was 'trailing lamely along at the back of the international pack'.

- Despite growing criticism from Europe, especially in Scandinavia, Britain again refused at the International Environment Conference in Munich in June 1984 to be committed to a 30 per cent cut by 1993. Apart from Greece and Ireland, Britain is the only European country that hasn't agreed.
- At a United Nations meeting in Geneva in September 1984, the Tories hedged again. Their pledge to reduce emission by 30 per cent by the end of the century was seen as too little, too

late. It fell far short of the new draft EEC Directive calling for a 60 per cent cut in sulphur and a 40 per cent cut in nitrogen oxide emission by 1995.

Friends of the Earth described the Tory contribution at Munich as 'At best a disappointing contrast to the positive spirit of international co-operation – at worst, a piece of pure effrontery.' The all-party Select Committee on the Environment, chaired by Hugh Rossi, demanded swift action on acid rain, including the recommendation that Britain should join the '30 per cent club' of nations committed to a 30 per cent reduction in emissions by 1993. Despite a plea by Hugh Rossi at last year's Tory Party Conference that 'time is running out', the government rejected the select committee's recommendations in December 1984.

Nuclear waste

The Tories will undoubtedly use growing concern about acid rain to back their case for expanding the nuclear energy programme. But while there are safe and relatively inexpensive ways of 'cleaning' flue gases from coal-fired power stations, no one has yet found a way of dealing safely with nuclear waste.

● A report prepared by Douglas Black, former president of the Royal College of Physicians, into the incidence of cancer near Britain's nuclear installations accepted that there could be a link between Sellafield's radioactive discharge and leukamia. A recent Yorkshire Television programme claimed that the leukemia rate for children living in the area was ten times the national average.

● Senior staff at British Nuclear Fuels were criticized, by the Nuclear Installations Inspectorate, in December 1983, for failing to deal early enough with a radioactive leak that had contaminated 25 miles of the Cumbrian coastline the previous month.

● The Irish government, together with a number of environmental pressure groups, has criticized the Tories for failing to keep the public better informed about radioactive discharges into the Irish Sea at Sellafield

The disposal of solid nuclear waste presents further problems, whether at sea or on land:

● The government was forced by TUC pressure to halt sea-dumping of low-level radioactive waste in December 1983, pending an independent inquiry into safety procedures. It has now accepted the inquiry report, published in December 1984, which recommended that sea dumping should cease until it can be shown that it is the 'best practicable environmental option'.

● An investigation by the Nuclear Industry Radioactive Waste Executive (NIREX) to dump intermediate-level waste at Billingham, Teeside, and Elstow, Bedfordshire, is being fiercely resisted by local inhabitants. In March this year, Imperial Chemical Industries at Billingham also announced its opposition to the investigation. The recent government announcement that Billingham will not be used for land dumping will only increase pressure on sites like Elstow. NIREX is now looking for five new land sites for nuclear waste.

In spite of this mounting public concern, the Tories have made it clear that they would like to privatize nuclear waste disposal. In February, the Department of the Environment invited tenders from private firms for a laboratory where research and development will be carried out. Plans to sell British Nuclear Fuels (BNFL) (which produces nuclear fuel, runs the reprocessing plant at Sellafield and deals with transportation of its irradiated fuel) are already under way, says the company's chief executive. Up to now, BNFL has been directly accountable to government. The £600,000 contract to deal with nuclear contamination at the Chatham dockyard has been awarded to a private company – NEI Nuclear Waste Technologies.

There is no evidence from the record of other sections of industry on pollution to quieten fears that making nuclear waste profitable and making it safe may conflict.

Lead in petrol

Lead is a deadly poison which can produce permanent brain damage in children. Yet every year some 7,500 tonnes of lead are emitted into the air in Britain from car exhausts.

The mental health of children can be adversely affected at relatively low levels of exposure. Studies show that lead causes distractability, hyperactivity and reduced IQ.

Despite the fact that three out of every four people questioned in a 1982 MORI poll said they would be prepared to pay more for lead-free petrol, the Tories have been painfully slow to take any action. Indeed, they have had to be dragged into reducing lead levels by the EEC.

● In 1981 they responded to the Select Committee on the Environment's report on lead by agreeing to comply with an EEC directive to reduce lead in petrol to 0.15 grammes per litre.

● However, West Germany reduced the level of lead in petrol to 0.15 grammes per litre nearly ten years ago. Now, with growing evidence of the effects of lead, the West Germans are looking to go further.

● In the Soviet Union, cars in cities and health resorts have run on lead-free petrol since 1959.

● Since 1975 all new cars in the USA have been required by law to take lead-free petrol. Most petrol now used in the USA is lead-free.

● In Japan, 95 per cent of petrol used is lead-free.

A new draft of EEC Directive calls on all member nations to sell lead-free petrol by 1986. By 1989 all new cars should be designed to run on unleaded petrol. On past evidence, Thatcher's Britain will be the last and slowest to comply. But there is no timetable for the *withdrawal* of leaded petrol. And since we don't known of any 'safe' level of blood lead, only a complete ban is acceptable.

In the meantime, children continue to be poisoned. The only effect of Tory policies is that they are being poisoned a little less quickly.

Pollution

The Tory record on pollution control is one of irresponsibility and neglect.

- Labour's Control of Pollution Act, due to be brought in in 1979, has still not yet been fully implemented. Cuts in council spending have left them, in some cases, unable even to do the basic paperwork. With inspectorates understaffed, proper enforcement will prove impossible.
- Controls over some hazardous and toxic wastes have been weakened.
- The power of the Secretary of State for the Environment to authorize disclosure of information on air pollution has been removed – giving polluters injustifiable protection from public scrutiny.
- The Clean Air Council has been abolished and provision in the Clean Air Acts relaxed.
- The Tories have led EEC resistance to US proposals that Europe follow their lead and ban the chloro-fluoro carbons in aerosols which, it is believed, deplete the ozone in our atmosphere.
- The Tories have abolished the Noise Advisory Council: work on controlling noise pollution is virtually at a standstill, despite the fact that most complaints received by the Environmental Health departments relate to noise.
- The ability of local authorities and government bodies to monitor and control pollution has been progressively curtailed by cuts in public expenditure.

The countryside

Each year under the Tories more and more of our countryside has been destroyed. Hedgerows have been ripped out. Moorlands have been ploughed up. Water courses have been polluted. And ponds have been drained. All in the pursuit of extra profits for already rich farmers; and all at a time when EEC food stores are bursting at the seams.

Under the Tories, and aided and abetted by the EEC's Common Agricultural Policy (CAP), Britain's farmers have abandoned the role they have claimed as custodians of the countryside. Now, as many seek to maximize their output and their profits to meet CAP objectives, they are perpetrating irreparable damage on the natural heritage which belongs to us all. The Tories have responded, but as usual inadequately.

They introduced the Wildlife and Countryside Act legislation which is riddled with loopholes and unworkable. They promised a freeze on prices of CAP products which are continually in surplus – and promptly broke their promise. They are cutting capital grants to farming. What they did was too little, too late. They have introduced legislation on pesticide safety – but it is wholly inadequate.

● **In 1981 the Wildlife and Countryside Act became law.** But it is ineffective and far too expensive to operate. It leaves vast tracts of countryside unprotected. And because of the loopholes in the Act, even those areas which should have been protected (the Sites of Special Scientific Interest) have suffered damage. The Nature Conservancy Council estimates that 20,000 acres of these prime sites are being lost or damaged each year.

● After considerable pressure, the government has announced that it will introduce **statutory controls on pesticides.** But nothing in the Bill suggests that the new legislation will be in any way adequate to deal with the problems that we currently face.

● Again in the face of considerable pressure, the Tories have announced **cuts in capital grants** to farming. These cuts – which have come about not out of any wish to protect the environment, but only as another means to cut public expenditure – will have no impact so long as the CAP remains unreformed and farmers continue to be encouraged to destroy the countryside in the pursuit of personal profit.

7. Culture

The Arts

■ *We should see to it that our people are steeped in a real knowledge and understanding of our national culture.*
Margaret Thatcher, May 1980

The subsidized arts are patronized by a tiny minority of people. But the Tories are intent on reducing access even further.

Under the first Thatcher administration, the arts got a bad deal. The future looks even bleaker:

● The amount of money spent on arts and libraries in real terms fell from £616 million in 1982–3 to £595 million in 1983–4 and is planned to fall to £544 million in 1984–5.
● The government-commissioned Priestley Report on the Royal Opera House and the Royal Shakespeare Company revealed that both are seriously underfunded. The report suggested that the companies be directly funded by Whitehall as opposed to the Arts Council. This would abandon the 'arm's length' principle which, rightly, protects the artistic independence of organizations.
● The cuts in 1981–2 left the Arts Council £10 million short of the minimum it needed and faced 40 organizations with loss of their grants.
● For 1985–6, Minister for the Arts Lord Gowrie has announced a 5.8 per cent overall increase in funds, but the basic rise for the Arts Council is limited to 3 per cent. Sir William Rees Mogg, who chairs the Arts Council, has warned that 'many of the council's clients, when faced with uplifts well below inflation, will find their very existence in jeopardy'.

'The Glory of the Garden'

The Arts Council strategy, as set out in its document 'The Glory of the Garden' (1984), shuffles around the existing limited budgets with no 'new' money forthcoming from government – robbing Peter to pay Paul. The new strategy will cost £6 million, but £5.5 million of this will be provided at the expense of existing clients – not through more government grant-in-aid.

Drama will be clobbered. This year 15 theatre companies will be robbed of the £1.2 million grants they received in 1984-5 (see Table 10).

The future of the Royal Court Theatre is uncertain. The theatre will continue to receive its grant for a further year.

Table 10.   Drama cuts

	Grant reduction (£)
Building-based companies	
Basingstoke: Horseshoe Theatre Company	72,000
Chester: Gateway Theatre Trust	87,500
Guildford: Yvonne Arnaud Theatre Management	108,000
London: Churchill Theatre Trust (Bromley)	90,500
Croydon Alternatives Theatre Company	73,500
Hornchurch Theatre Trust	148,000
King's Head Theatre Trust	55,000
Wakefield Tricycle Theatre Company	87,000
Harrogate (White Rose) Theatre Trust	132,500
Worthing and District Connaught Theatre Trust	76,000
Touring companies	
CAST Presentations	47,000
M6 Theatre Company	44,500
Mikron Theatre Company	28,500
7:84 Theatre Company (England)	92,500
Temba Theatre Company	72,000

But then it will be asked to find new funds from Tory-controlled Kensington and Chelsea Council, which has consistently refused to back it in the past. Sir Peter Hall, the National Theatre's director, has described the cuts as 'appallingly severe', necessitating the closure of the NT's smallest theatre, the Cottesloe.

Literature will be penalized. The council's literature budget is to be halved to £450,000. The National Book League's grant will be reduced by about a quarter. And there is a possibility that the government will impose VAT on books and newspapers.

Music will be cut. Funding for the four main London orchestras will be reduced. As much as £0.25 million will be withdrawn from the Opera 80 company.

National galleries and museums will be starved of funds. Their purchasing grants will be cut by an average of nearly 13 per cent. The director of the National Gallery, Sir Michael Levey, has stated: 'I am appalled and gravely perturbed by the implications of the minister's decision which can do nothing but restrict the National Gallery's activities and services to the public.'

Commercial sponsorship will be increased. Many of the Arts Council proposals depend on private sponsorship being able to make up the shortfalls with matching funds. But reliance on commercial sponsorship and 'venture capital' is precarious and largely limited to 'prestige' organizations and events.

The arts in the GLC and the metropolitan counties will be put at risk. As a result of the government's abolition proposals, many London boroughs and district councils would either be unwilling or unable to provide anything like the present level of support provided by the GLC and the metropolitan counties. Even the Arts Council called the proposals 'potentially damaging'. Lord Gowrie has been forced to find an extra £34 million for 1986 to help arts bodies in these areas. But since the grants to such bodies were expected to reach £38 million, this leaves £4 million for district and borough councils to find. Yet with penalties and rate-capping, it is highly unlikely that any extra local authority money for the arts will be found.

Tory proposals on local government will increase the centralization of the arts. Instead of elected councils distributing the money, £16 million would be given to the Arts Council to distribute to the main performing bodies at present subsidized by the GLC and the metropolitan counties – including London's South Bank. The remainder of the £34 million would be paid directly to museums and galleries in London, Manchester, Merseyside and Tyneside. Decision-making on the arts in these areas will be removed from elected councils and given to quangos.

Rate-capping and penalties will also cripple the arts in the provinces. Local authorities may be forced to cut non-statutory services like the arts. It will mean that many arts organizations and artists are in danger of losing their council grants and being unable to carry on their work.

Increasing political control
The Tories have increased their political control of the arts by appointing their political friends to key positions:

● Sir William Rees-Mogg, former editor of the *Times* and Margaret Thatcher's old ally, has been rewarded with the chair of the Arts Council.
● Luke Ritner has been appointed Secretary-General of the Arts Council. His only qualification is that he was previously administrator of the Association of Business Sponsorship for the Arts.

Films
In spite of the meagre public investment in the film industry, Britain has been able to produce a few Oscar-winning films such as *Chariots of Fire* and *Gandhi*. But instead of increasing funding for the production of more British films of this

quality, the government is to withdraw yet more public support and commitment from the film industry.

Capital allowances, as announced in the 1984 budget, have been terminated (see page 83). This leaves the industry without any form of tax incentive for investment at a time when the government's contribution is to be a paltry £10 million over five years.

The Films Bill will dismantle the machinery which underpins government support. The Bill:

● Abolishes the 'Eady levy' which attempted to redistribute the resources produced by the film industry as a whole, so that a proportion of its earnings are fed back to the film-makers. The levy system needed to be reformed, but there is to be no effective machinery to replace it.
● Sells off the National Film Finance Corporation (NFFC) which has done much to fund British films and which depends on Eady levy money. The government is planning to hand over the NFFC's assets to a private company.
● Abolishes the quota system which requires cinemas to show a minimum proportion of British films and guaranteed to the British industry a proportion of the British market and some protection against the flood of US imports.

Under the philistine Tories, Britain is in danger of becoming a cultural desert.

Cable TV

Cable TV licences were granted to 11 companies in November 1984. Major shareholders in some of the licences include British Telecom and Thorn-EMI. The licences will operate in a number of areas, including Aberdeen, Belfast, Coventry, Glasgow, Liverpool and London.

These, and future, licences will be operated by a new

Cable Authority, to be set up under the Cable and Broadcasting Act 1984. The Act also sets up a Satellite Broadcasting Board to supervise Direct Broadcast Satellite (DBS).

Since the publication of the Act in July 1984, Visionhire, a founder campaigner for cable TV, has withdrawn totally from the scheme, two further companies – British Telecom and Thorn-EMI – are reviewing their commitment in the light of gloomy market forces and the taxation changes made in the March 1984 budget, and BET (British Electric Traction) has sold its Rediffusion cable interests to Robert Maxwell.

The 1984 budget reduced capital expenditure allowances on plant and machinery (see page 83). These reductions have produced pessimism about cable TV, as has a report published by CIT Research in March 1984, which forecast that a mere 400,000 new homes would be added to cable TV by 1990.

In May 1984, a NEDC (National Economic Development Council) paper on cable TV argued that just 12,000 jobs would be created over a ten-year period. Only half of these would be permanent.

Direct Broadcast Satellite TV is now not expected to go into orbit until the end of 1988 – about two years late.

The Labour Party has criticised the Cable Act because:

● There is no quota on non-UK/EEC material.
● There is loose regulation of political bias and commercial interest in cable operations.
● There is a lack of support for UK equipment manufacturers.
● The Cable Authority is a completely unrepresentative body.

And in May 1984 the Director of the National Consumer Council warned that commercially sponsored programmes on cable TV could pose an 'insidious threat' to television standards. The threat lies in the potential for sponsors to influence the editorial content of programmmes. 'Will sponsored programmes especially made for cable,' he asked, 'be mixed with "normal" editorial and straight advertisements

193

on the same channel? If so, how will consumers be able to distinguish advertising from editorial matter?' It is essential for the maintenance of high television standards that editorial independence is safeguarded.

8. The changing face of politics

> ■ *If I won't work with Thatcher, why should I work with Thatcher with Brylcream?'*
>
> Neil Kinnock, Labour Party Conference,
> 2 October 1984

The pundits claim that Britain now has a three-party system. But, the Labour Party excepted, the choice facing British voters is one of style, not substance.

The new Tory Party

Under the leadership of Margaret Thatcher, the Tory Party has shifted far to the right. Once, Tories felt the need to show at least a degree of concern for those less fortunate than themselves. Such an approach is now scorned. Thatcher has made sure that the Conservative Party and the Conservative cabinet is dominated by 'yes men', who share her attitudes. Anyone who expresses dissent is given short shrift.

A right-wing cabinet

When Thatcher took office, 'traditional' Conservatives were well represented in the cabinet. During her first term, this gradually changed. Those who questioned the Prime Minister's doctrinaire approach were derided as 'wet'. Dissenting ministers such as Sir Ian Gilmour and Norman St John Stevas were sacked, while hard-line right-wingers like Norman Tebbit were promoted. This trend has continued since the 1983 general election. Almost immediately:

● Francis Pym, a leading moderate, was dismissed.

● Right-winger Nigel Lawson was made Chancellor of the Exchequer.
● Leon Brittan, former Chief Secretary to the Treasury, was promoted to Home Secretary.

The resignation of Cecil Parkinson during the party's 1983 conference brought Nicholas Ridley into the cabinet. Once described as 'Neanderthal', he was an advocate of Thatcherite economic policies long before Thatcher herself. In 1984 one of the few remaining moderates, James Prior, finding himself increasingly isolated, finally resigned.

The increasingly right-wing composition of the cabinet is reflected in the list of non-cabinet ministers and Parliamentary Private Secretaries – the next generation of Tory leaders. The Tories have now moved so far to the right that they have completely broken contact with the 'one nation' Tory Party of old. Indeed, the widespread presence of racists and extremists in Tory ranks is now a cause for concern.

Sinister elements within

It is now clear that extreme right-wing elements are increasingly active within the Tory Party. The party leadership, however, is doing next to nothing about the situation.

The evidence comes from within the Tory Party itself. Following reports of right-wing infiltration of some of their branches, the Young Conservatives began an inquiry which produced a report in September 1984. Conservative Central Office tried its best to avoid embarrassing publicity, but eventually an abbreviated ten-page report was released in January 1984. The report stated:

It is our considered opinion that a number of Conservative MPs are too closely connected with . . . extremist co-ordinating groups.

There are too many MPs who are prepared to use the questions of race and immigration in an emotive manner, whipping up bigotry and prejudice.

There are a number of Conservative councillors and ex-council candidates who were former members of the National Front and other right-wing groups.

We are led to the conclusion that extremist and racialist forces are at work inside the Conservative Party.

This disturbing report came after the disclosure that Tom Finnegan, Conservative candidate at Stockton South in the 1983 general election, was once a member of the National Front. And it followed calls for repatriation and the repeal of all race relations legislation at the 1983 Tory conference.

The Tory Party leadership has turned a blind eye to this mounting evidence. Many of the Young Conservatives' recommendations remain unimplemented. When questioned on BBC's *Panorama*, Tory Party chairman John Selwyn Gummer tried desperately to avoid the issue. When pressed, he asserted that 'the Tory Party is a totally non-racist party' and that there was insufficient evidence to warrant action.

Dissent and demise

The Tory Party has never been very tolerant of dissent in its ranks. The new Tory Party is even less so. Increasingly, Tories have found that the price of dissent is high. Naturally, these major splits in the party are never portrayed as such by the tame Tory press. But splits they are, none the less. So ruthless is the new Tory Party that dissent is usually voiced in code. But sometimes it emerges in less muted tones.

Francis Pym. Sacked after the 1983 election as Foreign Secretary – allegedly because he pointed to the dangers to the country of a possible Tory landslide – he has emerged as a major thorn in the side of the government. In a series of speeches, and in his book *The Politics of Consent*, he has berated the Tories remorselessly:

By far the most important issue both now and in the future for our people is employment. They adhere with notable rigidity to the economic policies prepared in the

1970s – the policies that were going to create 'real jobs'.
But it cannot be denied that those policies have not
yielded the results claimed for them. From the outset
. . . the government have consistently misjudged
unemployment. I believe that under present policies it
will continue to rise. (*Hansard*, 13 November 1984)

In *The Politics of Consent* he accuses Thatcher of having
turned herself into a president attempting to dictate the
policy of every Whitehall department. He describes her style,
and that of her government as 'narrow-minded', 'intolerant',
'absolutist', 'dogmatic', 'inflexible' and 'insensitive'.

Pym gives an indication of the extent to which the new
Tory Party has moved to the right:

I believe in a particular approach to politics which has
characterized the Conservative Party at its greatest
moments and has ensured its survival as a broad party of
government rather than as a narrow and dogmatic
faction.
    In time, the discarded notion that other people
might have a valid point of view will re-emerge.
Meantime, my concern is that the flag of traditional
Conservatism is kept flying . . . so that one day a
standard-bearer can pick it up and put it back at the
centre of our affairs, where it belongs.

Ian Gilmour. One of the earliest casualties of Thatcher's
policy of surrounding herself with 'yes men', he has spoken
out time and time again against the direction of the new Tory
Party. He has been most critical of Tory economic policy:

Far too often, this government has given the impression
that it does not sufficiently care about the unemployed
or about the plight of the poorer regions of the country.
    What has chiefly gone wrong is unemployment. it is
fear of unemployment which fuel the miners' strike . . .
Yet for many years the government has been claiming
that its policies were the only ones that could and would

create 'real' jobs. What has been the result? 'Real unemployment'. (*Guardian*, 26 September 1984)

It is not surprising that the new Tory Party has many fierce critics in local government in their own ranks.

George Tremlett. Former deputy-leader of the Tories on the GLC and one of the staunchest opponents of its abolition:

> My objections to the government's proposals to abolish the Greater London Council are fundamental. I believe they are a disgrace to parliament and bring shame upon the shoulders of the Conservative Party. My feelings are that strong because I know that the government is intent on forcing them through parliament for reasons that are immoral and intellectually insulting. The responsibility for this lies with the Prime Minister . . . Her reasoning is banal . . . She tolerates no opposition. (*City Limits*, 13 January 1984)

Roger Parker Jervis, who resigned, in disgust, from the chair of Buckinghamshire County Council.

> Right across the country prudent Conservative councillors know their targets are unrealistic and ridiculous, and that to spend above them is inevitable if local services are not to break down or become the subject of derision. Thus penalties will, as in Buckinghamshire, increasingly fall heavily on the same hapless ratepayers for whom the government claims to stand champion. I am not willing to countenance such injustice. (*Times*, 14 November 1984)

Finance from industry

As Tory links with farming and land-ownership weaken, so their links with big business are strengthened. Over the last six years the Tories have received, either directly or through various front organizations, at least £13 million from the coffers of industry. At a time when the Tories are imposing draconian restrictions on the political activities of trade unions, they totally reject any restrictions on the political activities of companies.

● In 1983–4 just over 30 companies accounted for nearly half the total amount donated to the Tory Party.

● There is increasing doubt about the legality of political donations made by companies. It seems that in most cases these payments are *ultra vires*. In any event, it is almost unheard of that the companies consult their shareholders, let alone their workforce, before making such payments.

● The overlap between who gets political honours and which companies give the Tories money seems to be growing.

● There is increasing concern within the Tory Party at the way in which its finances are handled. This disquiet found expression in a number of highly critical motions at a recent Conservative Central Committee meeting.

● The drive to privatize local council and NHS services has come at the same time as a massive increase in donations from companies who are tendering for these contracts.

● As well as the £13 million or so going to the Tory Party, another £1.1 million has been given by companies to a variety of organizations ranging from the SDP–Liberal Alliance to the right-wing extremists of Common Cause.

The Tories claim to be the party of proper housekeeping and standing on your own two feet. But when it comes to their own finances, their scruples fly right out of the window.

An undemocratic organization

■ *I believe in the two-party system and its inherent process of debate . . . Not so this Prime Minister. She tolerates no opposition.*

George Tremlett, *City Limits*, 13 January 1984

The structure of the Conservative Party exists mainly as a tool of the party leader, who has sole ultimate responsibility for developing policy and the manifesto. She is not accountable in any formal way to her party, and can change policy at whim.

The leader appoints all senior Conservative Party staff, including the chair of the party organization, the treasurer, and indeed all leading Central Office officials. Thatcher replaced all the top eight officials within one year. Former Chairman Cecil Parkinson was a close associate of Thatcher. His replacement, John Selwyn Gummer, is a political lightweight, appointed to carry out her orders.

The Conservative annual conference is little more than a talking shop: it has no rights or responsibilities. Resolutions and speakers are carefully pre-selected and whoever chairs the conference makes sure debates are safe. Resolutions are only 'advisory' to the leader. The platform has not been defeated for more than a decade. A Soviet official commented: 'This is just how we organize our conference' (*Observer*, 10 October 1982).

The Tory Party organization – the National Union – is a bureaucratic structure, designed to stifle discontent and manage debates. Its area offices are all controlled by Central Office appointees, and the local units – the Conservative Associations – have no channels by which they can individually or collectively influence party policy.

The SDP–Liberal Alliance: Tory Party mark II

The SDP–Liberal Alliance was formed in September 1981, some six months after the formation of the SDP. The Alliance has proved, by word and deed, that it is no friend of the labour movement:

● In February 1982 over 20 SDP and Liberal MPs voted with the Tories for the second reading of the Employment Bill. Only one SDP member voted with Labour against.
● In May 1982 eight Liberals voted for the third reading of the Employment Bill. The SDP members couldn't be bothered to vote.
● In April 1983 over 20 SDP and Liberal MPs voted with the Tories for the second reading of the Trade Union Bill. None

voted with Labour against the Bill. In April 1984, all the Liberal and SDP members abstained on the third reading of the Bill.

● Again in April 1983, seven Liberals and five SDP MPs voted with the Tories for a draft Code of Practice on the Closed Shop, based on the restrictive Employment Act 1980. None voted against with Labour.

● In April 1984 the SDP and Liberal members, with the support of 40 right-wing Tories, moved new clauses to the Trade Union Bill in an attempt to make it even more anti-union.

● The Labour Party's motion, in May 1984, condemning the government's decision to deploy cruise missiles was opposed by three SDP MPs, five Liberal MPs and the Tories. Two Liberals voted with Labour, one abstained and nine Liberal and three SDP members failed to turn up.

● In June 1984 no Liberal or SDP member supported Labour's motion opposing all nuclear bases in the UK.

● In July 1984 five SDP MPs and eleven Liberals voted with the Tories against a Labour censure motion on the NHS.

● In January 1985 six SDP MPs and 12 Liberals voted against a Labour censure motion on unemployment.

The SDP leaders in particular have nailed their colours firmly to the Tory mast. Their position on the miners' strike, for example, is no different from that of the Tories. The *Sunday Express* (15 July 1984) reported the ruminations of David Owen:

> If the miners' strike is lost it will be a dreadful blow to recovery and realism. It will not be just a defeat for Thatcher, but for the forces of sanity.

And in the *Financial Times* (8 September 1984):

> The Monopolies Commission demonstrates that 15 per cent of the industry accounted for £330 million of the losses. It's a devastating critique and it cannot be allowed to go on. This means that the pits will have to close.

The same *Financial Times* article further elucidates the Owen approach: 'There are aspects of Tory policy which I think have been a necessary realism.' It is hardly surprising that parallels have been drawn between Owen and Thatcher. On 12 February 1984, Walter Goldsmith, then Director-General of the Institute of Directors, could report a cosy rapport:

> When we had a meeting with Dr David Owen at the Institute, we found his thinking on most economic issues to be very much in line with free-market principles. It wasn't so clear what his members thought about this – but let me just say that Mrs Thatcher risks being outflanked on the right. If I were to be asked who were the two front-runners as the next Conservative Prime Minister, I should have to say Norman Tebbit and David Owen.

Owen's support for the social market economy was seriously criticized by the Liberal Party Council at a meeting on 2 December 1984. A motion passed by the council criticized 'Dr Owen's social market theories' and expressed concern that the SDP was 'placing too much faith in the market as a guarantor of individual rights'.

The SDP leader's right-wing views have brought the following comments from Ferdinant Mount, a top Tory journalist and a former Thatcher adviser (*Spectator*, 8 September 1984):

> Dr Owen's party-political problem is to distance himself from Mrs Thatcher while holding to most of her policies . . . Where he differs with the government on practical matters, it is because he takes a tougher line.

Mount's review of David Owen's book, *A Future That Will Work*, continued:

'This book could be safely put into the hands of the most rabid Thatcherite without causing him or her a moment's discomfort.'

The Alliance: divided on policy

Despite the apparent unity of the Alliance in terms of support for Tory policies, there are, however, clear signs of growing rifts between and within the two parties.

Defence. The Liberal Party, unlike its parliamentary leadership, is opposed to the deployment of cruise missiles. The SDP both as a party and in parliament is in favour of the deployment of cruise. The Liberals' 1984 Assembly, against the wishes of David Steel, voted for the immediate removal of cruise missiles. The SDP Assembly didn't even debate the subject. In October 1984 SDP defence spokesperson, John Cartwright, called for sea-launched cruise missiles to replace Britain's Polaris when it becomes obsolete in the 1990s.

Nuclear Power. The Liberal Party opposes the development of nuclear power. The SDP supports the development of nuclear power.

Health. The Liberals support the principle of a free health service and are opposed to keeping charges for health. But the SDP would keep them.

Devolution. In March 1984, the SDP endorsed plans for a Welsh assembly in Cardiff. A month later, the Liberals rejected a proposal for a grand council for Wales.

Local government. The SDP proposed the abolition of the GLC and the metropolitan counties in 1983. Yet the Liberals are opposed to their abolition. To add to the confusion, an Alliance document published in September 1984 said that, in the long term, the GLC must be incorporated into a new form of government, with additional regional responsibilities.

Plastic bullets. In September 1984 the SDP's policy-making Council for Social Democracy passed a motion against the use of plastic bullets in Northern Ireland. Less than a month later, the leadership's policy committee overturned the decision. The Liberals are opposed to the use of plastic bullets.

The squabble over seats

The differences in philosophy between the Liberals and SDP leaders and the aggressive competitiveness of the latter led to major rows over the division of seats for the 1983 general election and the 1984 European elections. This forced many Liberals to question the future of the Alliance. In a letter to the *Times* (18 November 1984), former Liberal Party president Richard Holme stated: 'Your [*Times*] leader is right in one respect when it says that the two Alliance parties "are if anything, growing further apart as the post-election weeks pass".'

The argument over the division of seats during the period prior to the European elections prompted John Pardoe, former deputy-leader of the Liberal Party, to comment: 'If the SDP can't survive without stars, it hasn't got a future. It has always been a party from and for the top, with too many chiefs and not enough Indians' (*Sunday Times*, 1 April 1984).

The Liberals want joint selection of candidates by members of both parties, but are not willing to divide up constituencies with the SDP as they did for the 1983 general election. The SDP nationally do *not* want joint selection, and favour the division of seats on an equal basis. An even division of seats would, of course, benefit the SDP because of its smaller membership both inside and outside parliament. A division according to numerical strength would distribute the seats approximately three to one in the Liberals' favour.

In October 1984 the Welsh council of the SDP put a spanner in the works by reaffirming an electoral agreement with the Welsh Liberal Party, providing for joint selection by members of both parties of candidates in 13 of the 38 Welsh parliamentary seats. A month later the two leaders – David Steel of the Liberals and David Owen of the SDP – made an unsuccessful attempt to patch up the differences between the two parties. A statement issued following a meeting on 20 November said:

Joint selection may be undertaken in exceptional circumstances where helpful and appropriate as was done in the European elections, but cannot be widespread, and we hope that in most seats our parties will proceed expeditiously to implement the existing agreement.

The existing agreement means that neither party gets what it wants. Thus, the two sides are about as far apart as ever. The day after the statement the *Financial Times* commented: 'The wording is carefully phrased to sooth the sensibilities of the various factions within the Alliance.'

David Owen, of course, favours an equal distribution of seats. This would strengthen the SDP and improve his prospects of becoming undisputed leader of the Alliance. But neither party can agree on a merger. So, for the moment, he has to be content with moulding the SDP in his own likeness. William Wallace, a leading Liberal academic, has described the SDP 'as a party with a leader who preaches a decentralist philosophy but prefers to practice democratic centralism' (*New Society*, 22 September 1983).

It is not, therefore, surprising that the Liberals and the SDP continue to operate as two separate parties.

9. Britain in the world

The EEC budget: a very transparent deal

Foreign Office minister Malcolom Rifkind called it 'a major success for Britain' (*Times*, 29 June 1984). Others thought differently. The *Economist* (7 July 1984) commented:

> It was neither a permanent settlement of the budget nor did it embrace a fundamental reform of the Common Agricultural Policy. It was merely another, slightly better, slightly less temporary deal reducing Britain's budget contributions, won by cashing in one of Britain's two main EEC bargaining levers – no increase in the community's revenue.

And as the dust settles, the loose ends are picked up and the final details worm their way out, it is plain for all to see that Thatcher's deal, far from being a success, is an out-and-out failure. A failure that will cost Britain dearly.

After five years of sabre-rattling, **the Tories have failed to reform the EEC budget.** Over two-thirds is still spent on supporting farmers while only a tiny fraction is used to help industry. Perhaps we should not have expected anything else. The Tories have always seen budget reform as nothing more than another cost-cutting exercise, another attempt to cut public expenditure, another source of tax cuts for the rich.

The UK's excessive contributions to the EEC must be seen in their proper light. They reflect the fact that **the EEC is more concerned with building butter mountains than it is with creating jobs.** And that poses a real dilemma for the Tories. For they, too, are more concerned with lining the pockets of rich farmers (witness Peter Walker's record as

Minister of Agriculture) than they are with solving the problem of mass unemployment. The dilemma was bound to lead to failure in the budget negotiations. The budget deal is a failure because:

It is a temporary solution. Despite the Tory rhetoric, this deal will last only as long as the deal to increase member states' VAT contributions lasts. As part of the budget deal, the VAT take is to be increased from 1 per cent to 1.4 per cent. All the experts agree that the increase will be able to supply the EEC with sufficient funds only for the next two or three years. So by 1986 Britain will be back at the negotiating table.

It has done nothing to curb farm spending. In presenting the deal, the Tories talked about 'measures to guarantee effective budgetary discipline'. But the government sacrificed any attempt to put a curb on farm spending in their rush to get the 1983 rebate of £460 million. Instead, the Tories accepted a deal which, in the words of the *Financial Times* (2 October 1984), 'falls short of the legally binding package sought by the UK'.

Worse still, the deal allows the Council of Ministers 'flexibility' to exceed the proposed limits on farm spending in the event of 'abnormal developments' or if 'ministers agree to do so'. And the decisions to exceed the limits will be taken on a 'qualified majority' – so that Britain will be unable to veto any increase in spending.

The weakness of the deal was highlighted by *Farmers' Weekly* (30 November 1984): 'Farmers have nothing to fear from the EEC budget discipline agreement drawn up in Brussels to control the Common Agricultural Policy because it is so full of escape clauses.'

It leaves unresolved the budget deficits for 1984 and 1985. The 1984 budget is overspent by over £1 billion while the budget for 1985 has a planned overspend of about £1.6 billion. So much for budgetary discipline — but it also means that the money to pay the UK's 1984 rebate of £600 million (which is due in 1985) will not be available. Another fight seems certain!

It leaves Britain paying more than in the past. As a result of a combination of the EEC's creative accountancy and Tory backsliding, the rebates the government secured with this 'permanent' deal are less than they have been:

● In the past, Britain has been getting back about two-thirds of its net contributions.

● In 1984 our rebate was less than half our planned net contribution (before taking account of any measures to pay for the overspend).

● From 1985 onwards our rebate will be calculated on the basis of a new assessment of our contribution – an assessment which will mean that our rebate will again be less than half of our real net contribution.

At the end of the day, there can be only one way to describe this deal – a sell-out. It's going to cost us money. It's not permanent. It does nothing about farm spending. After five years of conflict the Tories have achieved nothing.

Third World debt; another year of living dangerously

In recent years there have been growing fears of a financial collapse in the developing world, a collapse which would engulf rich and poor countries alike. Experts have urged Western governments to take prompt, even drastic, action.

The situation is this: the debt problem was born ten years ago. The oil price rise of 1973–4 drastically changed world economic conditions. It meant that non-oil-producing countries, like Brazil, had to cut back on their essential imports or greatly expand their export earnings to pay for higher oil costs. Recession and monetarist policies in the advanced industrial countries made it more difficult for the non-oil developing countries to win their biggest markets. Every year more trade barriers have been erected against the exports of the non-oil developing countries, so only a few of these countries managed to export their way out of trouble. The rest found it impossible to cut their imports sufficiently – so they borrowed from abroad and hoped that economic growth in the future would enable them to pay their debts.

Non-oil-producing developing countries buy one-fifth of world imports. Since 1981, commodity prices of basic raw materials and foodstuffs have fallen sharply, cutting their incomes. Loan interest payments increased as world interest rates rose and their debts soared by more than $100 billion dollars to $370 billion.

Annual repayments by the top 25 debtors alone were expected to rise from $35 billion in 1984 to $85 billion in 1987 (*South*, August 1984). Brazil's debts are $93 billion, Mexico's $90 billion and Nigeria's $15 billion.

● Over $20 billion is currently owed to UK financial institutions from just seven countries. In Britain, Stock Market fears about the Midland Bank's loans to Latin America led to a fall in its share value from £4 to £2.77 between April and June 1984.

● In the USA, Continental Illinois was kept in business only through an unprecedented government rescue package. The share value of another major US bank, Manufacturers' Hanover, fell by 11 per cent *in one day* in May 1984 following news about loan repayment problems.

So, in June 1984 the Third World's eyes were fixed on the London Seven-Nation Economic Summit in the hopes that action would be taken. But they were to be disappointed. All Thatcher produced were vague statements on 'terrorism' and 'democracy' – nothing constructive or relevant.

At the time Sir Geoffrey Howe described any moves towards a more collective management of the international economic system as 'an intellectual trap'. The seven nations at the Summit produced no solutions. They simply tinkered with debt rescheduling and agreed that the International Monetary Fund (IMF) should play a 'central role', thus laying themselves open to the charge that the summit's 'response to this deflationary, and potentially disastrous, situation has clearly been to opt for small improvements to existing safety-nets rather than attempt through-going reform' (*Guardian*, 11 June 1984).

The seven nations participating in the summit control 46 per cent of the votes at the IMF. The IMF has attached tough conditions to its loans to debtor countries. These have included the repayment of debts as they fall due, major cuts in imports, raising consumer prices on essential goods such as oil, cutting public spending, halting new development projects, allowing more direct foreign investment and renewing the drive for export earnings.

The IMF has given no help on negotiating cheaper loans or tackling such major development problems as low prices for the exported products of the non-oil developing countries. The IMF approach has been pursued on a strictly case-by-case basis.

All the major debtor countries have been forced to accept the IMF's conditions. If the conditions are accepted, then the commercial banks also make new loans.

Yet by the beginning of 1984 the major debtor countries had had enough. IMF austerity programmes were proving politically unpopular and economically damaging. Mexico's total production had dropped 4 per cent in a year. Brazil was paying over half of its export earnings in debt repayments. Nigeria had to pay about 20 per cent of its export earnings on interest on foreign debts, while Togo and the Ivory Coast had to pay more than 50 per cent.

By September 1984 Chancellor Lawson, addressing the IMF's annual meeting, faced demands from the Third World, and particularly the Commonwealth, to throw Britain's weight behind a programme of global recovery. There were calls for lower interest rates and for the IMF and the banks to drop their deflationary country-by-country approach to debt problems. Lawson did not seem concerned by the mounting problems; he thrust his head further into the sand:

> We have to persevere with the present approach . . .
> There is no sensible alternative to the case-by-case
> approach which we have been pursuing. Contrary to
> what is alleged by its critics, it represents a coherent
> strategy.

In his response to the Commonwealth secretariat report to the Toronto finance ministers' meeting in September 1984, Lawson ignored its constructive ideas. He talked about the need for third world governments to moderate their calls on the world's savings stock held by the rich countries to prevent rising interest rates. This is a bizarre new approach to justify the same policy that the Tory Party has been peddling in Britain in the last five years. Lawson totally fails to distinguish the use which governments can make of these savings to rebuild their economics from the speculative and unproductive uses to which much of the world's financial system is designed to put them.

The Tories stubbornly resist any long-term, coherent strategy. Such a strategy could:

- Place the debt problem within the responsibility of a restructured World Bank and IMF.
- Encourage new contributions from oil-rich states.
- Expand trade between the developed and developing countries.
- Stabilize commodity prices and interest rates to end the drain on third world resources.
- Help to build new industry in the Third World.

Thatcher and the Third World: while millions starve

■ *There is a genuine argument about what all the aid programmes – bilateral and multilateral – are really achieving; and at times the disappointments can loom large and the measurable achievements look rather thin.*

Timothy Raison, Minister for Overseas
Development, *British Overseas Aid 1983*

Raison has indeed a lot to be humble about when he tries to draw up a list of Tory achievements in the field of third world development. In a world still ravaged by mass poverty, still reeling from the recession which monetarist policies induced, Tory Britain has been a beacon of heartlessness, a shining example of callous indifference towards the millions who starve.

Aid quantity: the unkindest cut of all

The level of overseas aid spending, never in itself a complete answer to mass poverty, is nevertheless a good barometer of any government's concern for the third world. The United Nations recommends that each Western nation should give 0.7 per cent of its Gross National Product (GNP) in aid each year. But British aid spending under the Tories has shown an unremitting decline (figures as a percentage of GNP):

- 1979 – 0.52
- 1980 – 0.35
- 1981 – 0.43
- 1982 – 0.37
- 1983 – 0.35

However, the GNP measure tells only half the story about the appalling Tory record on aid volume. In May 1984, Timothy Raison was asked in parliament to provide aid figures since 1979 and forecast aid spending to 1985 in fixed monetary values (according to the value of the pound in 1979). Raison replied that aid expenditure had fallen from £836 million in 1978–9, to £696 million in 1983–4 – a drop of some 17 per cent. In other words, the Tories have reserved the most vicious of all their public spending cuts for the aid budget in 1985–6.

Tory apologists insist that an increase in aid spending

depends on economic recovery in Britain. But while Nigel Lawson regularly announces that Britain's recovery is under way, our aid spending continues to slip ever downwards. The Tories have also conveniently ignored the commitment set down in the 'Economic Declaration' of the London summit:

> to maintain and wherever possible increase flows of resources, including official development assistance . . . to the developing countries and particularly to the poorest countries.

The Thatcher government plainly has no intention of carrying out this pledge.

A number of other countries take their aid obligations rather more seriously than Tory Britain. Even some non-socialist governments have managed to provide creditable levels of aid in difficult economic circumstances. The abysmal Tory performance on aid spending in GNP percentage terms becomes all the more marked when set against the performances of some European neighbours.

- France **increased** spending from 0.73 per cent GNP in 1981 to 0.75 and 0.76 in the following two years.
- Germany **increased** spending from 0.47 per cent GNP in 1981 to 0.48 and 0.49 in the following two years.
- Sweden **increased** spending from 0.83 per cent GNP in 1981 to 1.02 and 0.88 in the following two years.

Meanwhile, Britain is set to spend a miserable £1,100 million (O.35 per cent of GNP) in the financial year 1984–5 – a sum equivalent to less than a tenth of the likely cost of the Trident missile system. Such are the spending priorities of Thatcher's Britain.

Aid quality: cheating the poor

But, of course, aid volume is not the whole story; the *quality* of aid is vital. Yet a great deal of Tory aid has not served the needs of poor people. During the course of 1982 and 1983, for example, the Tories spent over £140 million of taxpayers money through the Aid Trade Provision. The provision is a device by which aid money is offered to third world governments which are considering tenders from British firms for particular projects. Funding through the provision has been not unreasonably described as a system of bribes. It is governments – often corrupt governments – rather than people which benefit from the provison's transfers. In 1982 and 1983, Paraguay, one of the worst dictatorships in South America, received over £4 million through this scheme.

Moreover, the Tory government makes no connection between aid spending and human rights. Many governments which cannot be trusted to treat their own citizens decently have enjoyed lavish Tory generosity. For example, savage abuse of human rights has not prevented the Tories from putting over £20 million in gross aid into the coffers of the regime in Ankara in the years 1982 and 1983. Poor people in Turkey should not expect to benefit from this money. For his part, Timothy Raison feels a bit shy about raising difficult questions about aid and human rights. In July 1984 he was asked whether, while visiting the country, he had questioned the authorities in Pakistan (to which Britain provided £16 million in 1983) over human rights abuse. He replied:

> The question of human rights abuse was not raised during my visit. I am confident that the Pakistan government are in no doubt that we deplore violations of human rights wherever they occur.

So Timothy Raison, Britain's minister with responsibility for the third world, has too much on his mind to raise human rights violations with foreign governments.

Central America: running after Ronnie

Central America is a region characterized by corrupt and repressive regimes, by appalling poverty and by violent conflicts.

Since he took office, President Reagan has treated the area as his own backyard: a place where American influence must dominate, whatever the wishes of the local people. His policies have exacerbated the region's problems and have associated the USA with political forces hostile to democracy and to human rights. In spite of all the evidence to the contrary, President Reagan maintains that Central America is the scene of an attempt by Moscow-manipulated communists to take over. This delusion may yet induce the President to commit US troops in a full-scale war.

Almost alone among the NATO allies, the Thatcher government has slavishly followed President Reagan as he has plunged the USA deeper into the quagmire of his Central American policies. At Reagan's bidding, Britain sent observers to the bogus elections in El Slavador in 1982 and 1984 in order to help legitimize the result in the eyes of the world opinion. The British government did this in spite of the fact that:

● Many democratic parties were unable to campaign openly for fear of being annihilated and boycotted the poll – an action with which even the Tories' observers had to sympathize.
● According to the most authoritative non-governmental source, over 5,200 civilians were slaughtered in El Salvador in 1983 – mostly at the hands of right-wing death squads.

At the same time, again at Ronnie's command, the Thatcher administration has opposed the Sandinista government in Nicaragua – which Ronald Reagan says is under 'a communist reign of terror' – in spite of the fact that:

● The CIA has been financing a covert war against Nicaragua from Costa Rica and Honduras: Nicaraguan ports have been mined with Washington's full complicity.
● The Sandinistas have introduced democracy into Nicaragua; they have extended health-care and education; aid agencies are on record as saying the the Sandinistas have made a huge effort to improve living standards.

Also in Central America, the democracy of Belize is

threatened by territorial claims from the vile dictatorship of General Mejia Victores in Guatemala. Belize looks to Britain to guarantee its security – yet this is another commitment from which the Tories are beginning to back away. Of Britain's small garrison in Belize, Tory minister Ray Whitney, speaking in the Commons on 31 July 1984, said: 'We naturally wish to see as soon as possible conditions in which it can be safely withdrawn.'

In other words, Belize is soon to be left at the mercy of the regime with the worst human rights record in Central America.

The Falklands: facing down the future

The Thatcher government is not even bothering to think about the long-term future of the Falkland Islands. Instead, it is persisting with its absurd 'Fortress Falklands' policy. This policy has already cost £3,000 million.

Even after the new runway (costing £240 million) is completed in 1986, Fortress Falklands will cost £450 million in 1986–7 and £300 million in 1987–8 – £1.5 million per annum for every Falklands family.

The Thatcher government currently bases 4,000 British troops on the Falkland Islands. A quarter of the Royal Navy's frigates and destroyers are tied up in defence of Fortress Falklands. For its part, Argentina has re-equipped its forces which are now more modern and effective than they were in 1982. To the Argentine military, Fortress Falklands will serve merely as needling provocation.

Since the Falklands war, British relations with Argentina have not been normalized. Thatcher has set her face against any discussions on the sovereignty of the Falklands. It was her obstinacy on this point that caused the breakdown of the tentative negotiations which took place in Berne in July 1984 between British and Argentine officials.

Thatcher plainly believes that she does not have to discuss sovereignty because she 'won' the war. It's worth now recalling that just prior to the reinvasion of the Falklands in

1982, Tory propaganda made much of the fact that Britain was prepared to accept:

- a United Nations presence on the islands;
- the resumption of *unconditional* negotiations on the future of the islands under the auspices of the UN Secretary-General.

Nowadays though, Thatcher is determined to block all progress on the sovereignty issue; just as she is determined to ignore the pressing need to protect the real interests of the islanders in the years ahead. Fortress Falklands is not just a monumental failure of statecraft – it's a costly way of storing up trouble for the future.

Now that Sir Geoffrey Howe has secured, in his words, 'an historic and remarkable' agreement with communist China over the future of Hongkong, surely it is time for a fraction of the same diplomatic effort to be put into securing a durable solution to the Falklands problem?

Defence

Despite the ever-increasing threat of nuclear annihilation, the Tories are continuing with their expensive and dangerous nuclear arms build-up. The deployment of cruise missiles, the decision to purchase Trident and cuts in Britain's real conventional defences all threaten the security of this country. Tory defence policy also threatens the jobs of thousands of defence industry workers.

Cruise missiles

In the face of huge public opposition, the first 'flight' of 16 US ground-launched cruise missiles arrived at Greenham Common in November 1983. In November 1984 it was announced by the American Supreme Allied Commander Europe, General Bernard Rogers, that another 16 cruise missiles had arrived at Greenham. The Tory government had given no advance warning of this either to parliament or to the British people.

A total of 96 cruise missiles are planned for Greenham by

1986. Construction of the Molesworth base started in spring 1985 and a further 64 cruise missiles are due to be deployed there by 1988.

Despite government and Tory local authority harassment, the four-year-old Greenham Peace Camp has been maintained and cruise convoys have been tracked and followed when they go out on 'exercises'.

Arms negotiations

The nuclear arms negotiations in Geneva broke down in late 1983 and the Soviet Union deployed nuclear missiles as 'counter-measures' in East Germany and Czechoslovakia. The USA deployed its first sea-launched cruise missiles in June 1984. This was swiftly followed by an announcement of deployment of Soviet 'cruise' missiles on bombers and submarines.

During Labour leader Neil Kinnock's visit to Moscow in November 1984, it was announced that the USA and USSR would have exploratory talks about resuming arms negotiations in January 1985. New negotiations will commence in Geneva in March 1985. However, there is little prospect of an early success.

Trident: a threat to Britain and arms control

The British government's decision to purchase the Trident nuclear submarine missile system is disastrous.

● Trident will increase British and NATO dependence on highly accurate nuclear 'warfighting' weaponry designed not for old-fashioned 'deterrence' but for a 'first-strike' capability. Trident represents a unilateral escalation of the number of independent targets Britain could destroy from 64 with Polaris to between 512 and 896 with Trident II.

● Trident will damage prospects for future arms control negotiations between the Warsaw Pact and NATO. Exclusion of Britain's Polaris from the negotiations was a major factor in the failure of the 1983 Geneva talks. The Russians argued, with justification, that all NATO nuclear weapons targeted against the USSR – *including* those of Britain and

France – should be taken into account in the negotiations.

● Trident is not really 'independent' of the USA, in any case. Like Polaris, it will be targeted by US satellites and use US computers at Omaha, Nebraska. Trident missiles will be serviced at Kings Bay, Georgia. Purchase of Trident ties us into US technology and strategy for the next 40 years.

● The vast expenditure on Trident is damaging to our real conventional defences, particularly Britain's surface fleet.

● Trident undermines the Nuclear Non-Proliferation Treaty by encouraging other countries to follow Britain's bad example.

Trident is not independent. It is not British and it will not deter. Its possession provides Britain with either an expensive, but useless, status symbol, or a guaranteed weapon of national suicide, should any government be so foolish as to attempt to use it.

NATO's deep-strike offensive

In 1982 the US Army unilaterally adopted a new doctrine called 'AirLand Battle'. The British government has confirmed that AirLand Battle will apply to all US Army forces world-wide including those in Britain (*Hansard*, 13 March 1984). This doctrine envisages use of chemical, nuclear and conventional forces in an 'integrated battlefield'. US forces in Europe have taken part in exercises based on AirLand Battle doctrine.

The US pressurized its NATO allies to adopt a new military strategy known as 'Follow-on Force Attack' (FOFA), which is similar to AirLand Battle and, like it, involves 'deep strike' into Eastern Europe. Without consultation with parliament, this proposal to change NATO strategy was agreed to by Britain's representatives on NATO's military committee and Britain's Ambassador to NATO. It was formally endorsed by NATO defence ministers in December 1984. This new strategy marks a significant shift towards an offensive warfighting posture for NATO based upon new, largely American, 'emerging technology' (ET) weapons.

New civil defence regulations

New civil defence regulations came into effect in December 1983. They give the government power to enforce regulations and centralize control of nuclear war planning. They foster the myth that there can be effective civil defence against a direct nuclear attack.

Defence spending crisis: cuts to come

The Conservative government faces a mounting crisis in its defence budget with the likelihood of big cuts in the real defence of Britain, the Royal Air Force, the British Army of the Rhine and the Navy. According to a report in the *Daily Telegraph* (10 October 1984):

> By 1986, if its own public expenditure plans are to be believed, the govenment will end its commitment to increase defence spending by 3 per cent in real terms each year. If the Treasury has its way, defence spending will actually begin to decline.

Part of the problem is escalating equipment costs. The proportion of the British defence budget spent on equipment has risen from 34 per cent to 46 per cent in nine years. Other reasons are the escalating costs of Trident and the costs of the Fortress Falklands policy. Defence expenditure in cash terms has more than doubled from £9,228 million in 1979/80 to a planned total of £18,870 million in 1987/8.

The cost of Trident

The estimated cost of Trident over a 15-year period has doubled from £5,000 million in 1980 prices to an officially estimated £9,400 million in May 1984 prices (House of Commons Defence Select Committee). The falling value of the pound against the US dollar is one factor. Half the total cost of Trident is to be spent in the USA on US missiles and technology. However, the official costings are widely criticized as an underestimate. Various independent observers put the cost of Trident at already up to £12,000 million at 1984 prices (see M. Chalmers, 'Trident', CND, 1984). By the late

1980s Trident and Polaris will be costing some 15 per cent of the total defence budget.

Many prominent military figures, and increasing numbers of Conservative politicians, now favour the abandonment of Trident. The Liberal Party and the SDP are also opposed to Trident on cost grounds, although the latter favour an alternative nuclear weapon system, the dangerous submarine-launched cruise missiles which are almost impossible to verify.

The peak years for Trident expenditure will be 1987–93 at a time when the real defence budget will be falling, thereby exerting great pressure for cuts in Britain's real conventional defences. As the *Daily Telegraph* reported on 10 October 1984:

> Mr Heseltine is going to have to decide whether he wants to cancel Trident, implement naval cuts which go a great deal further than Sir John Nott would have dared envisage in 1981, or find a way of reducing the Rhine Army by 50 per cent which will not drive our NATO allies into apoplexy.

Jobs losses for defence workers

Under the Tories there have been closures and job losses for defence workers. Chatham Dockyard was closed, Plymouth and Portsmouth reduced. Aerospace workers face insecurity and the number of Ministry of Defence civil servants has been slashed. The privatization of the Royal Ordnance Factories and the 'Levene Proposals' for the Royal Dockyards threaten the jobs of thousands.

The Tories have made no plans for conversion or alternative employment for communities hit by their policy.

Heseltine plans to cut the number of defence civil servants from 209,000 to 168,000. Part of this cut is due to the statistical trick of transferring 18,500 workers out of the public sector, with the privatization of the Royal Ordnance Factories. Other cuts will be caused by a restructuring of the Ministry of Defence, 'a comprehensive management reorganization', and the establishment of a new Combined Defence Staff under General Sir John Stanier. Finances of the Services will come under a new Office of Management and Budget.

Mrs Thatcher's diary

May 1979

3 May: Tories win general election.
Jobs lost: ICI 1,200 over three years.

June 1979

First Tory budget. Basic rate of VAT up from 8 to 15 per cent.

Top rate of income tax down from 83 to 60 per cent and basic rate down from 33 to 30 per cent. Spending cuts of £2.8 billion.

Minimum Lending Rate up from 12 to 14 per cent.

Scotland and Wales Acts repealed, ending any plans for devolution.

Jobs lost: Inland Revenue 1,000.

July 1979

Cuts of over one-third in regional aid announced.

Price Commission abolished.

British Aerospace to be denationalized.

Energy Commission disbanded.

Education Act passed – allowing LEAs to continue selection.

Regional planning councils to be disbanded.

Jobs lost: British Steel 12,000.

August 1979

British Shipbuilders announce cuts of 10,000 jobs in merchant shipbuilding within 18 months.

Jobs lost: Perkins Diesel 7,000, Chrysler 2,000, Hoover 700–1,200.

September 1979

Post Office to be split into two separate corporations.

School meals charges increased from 25p to 30p.

Overseas student fees raised by 32 per cent.

Urban development corporations to be set up in London and Merseyside Docklands.

Fifty-seven 'quangos' axed.

Jobs lost: BL 25,000, Prestcold 1,000, GKN 1,000, ITT 900, Courtaulds 600.

October 1979

Exchange controls abolished.

Public stake in BP reduced from 51 to 46 per cent.

Jobs lost: Singer 3,000, International Computers 1,200.

November 1979

Public spending cuts of £3,500 million announced for 1980–1.

NEB Board resigns en bloc.

Protection of Official Information Bill abandoned after widespread criticism.

Interest rates up to a record 17 per cent.

Jobs lost: 40,000 civil service jobs to go over three years, Courtaulds 2,600, British Steel 2,000, ICI 2,000 Talbot 1,500, Massey Ferguson 1,500, Firestone 1,500, BSR 1,000.

December 1979

National Ports Council abolished.

National Enterprise Board sells public stake in ICL.

Expansion of nuclear power programme announced.

Five per cent devaluation of 'green pound'.

New immigration rules approved.

Jobs lost: Harland and Wolff 1,200.

January 1980

Mortgage rate goes up to all-time record of 15 per cent.

Abandonment of 'Parker Morris' minimum standards for new council housing announced.

Jobs lost: British Steel 11,300, Lesney Products 7,500, Leyland Vehicles 750.

February 1980

School meal charges increased from 30p to 35p.

Manpower Services Commission budget cut by an additional £30 million a year from 1981.

Governement-commissioned report published suggesting break-up of ILEA (report rejected).

Funds for housing investment cut by a third.

Jobs lost: Laird Group 1,500, Massey Ferguson 1,000, Tootal 800.

March 1980

Tories' second budget. Sets out financial plans for spending cuts and monetary restraint over four years.

Public expenditure White Paper announces plans to halve public spending on housing between 1979–80 and 1983–4, and cut education expenditure by 9.5 per cent.

Enterprise Zone proposal announced.

Jobs lost: Laird 1,500.

April 1980

Prescription charges raised from 45p to 70p.

Education Act passed.

Jobs lost: Lucas Electrical 1,000, Courtaulds 750.

May 1980

Rate of inflation reaches 21.9 per cent — more than double the May 1979 level.

British Aerospace Act lays plans for privatization.

Ian MacGregor appointed to chair of British Steel Corporation with 'transfer fee' of up to £1.8 million.

Jobs lost: Courtaulds 12,300, NCB 4,200, BCS 3,600, Talbot 1,300.

June 1980

Announcement of UK sites for 160 cruise missiles.

Gas Act.

Industry Act forces NEB asset sales.

Jobs lost: Lucas Electrical 3,000, Ilford 2,500, BSR 2,300, Ford 2,300, GKN 2,000, Alfred Herbert 1,343, Grundig

1,000, Burton 750, Levey Products 750, Courtaulds 660.

July 1980

Arms embargo on Chile lifted.

Sales of National Enterprise Board stake in Ferranti announced.

Weakening of the Post Office and Telecommunications monopolies announced.

Government announces decision to spend £5,000 million on Trident I as Polaris replacement.

Enterprise Zone sites announced.

Transport Act passed.

Announcement of setting up of holding company to 'privatize' British Rail subsidiaries.

Jobs lost: National Freight Corporation 1,100, Perkins 650, John Dickinson 630, BL Components 580.

August 1980

Unemployment goes over 2 million for first time in 45 years.

Employment Act restricts trade union rights.

Housing Act.

Government announces extra £45 million for civil defence for period 1981/2–1983/4.

Jobs lost: John Ayers 1,900, Bowater 1,600, Courtaulds 1,200, Reed Paper and Board 700, Massey-Ferguson 680, Hoover 440.

September 1980

Government announces £200 million cut in local authority grants for 1980–1, with extra penalties for 'high-spending' councils.

British Rail and National Bus Company announce service cuts.

Jobs lost: CEGB 3.000, Girling 2,200, GKN 2,000, Metal Box 1,260, Royal Doulton 1,000, Courtaulds 700, BP Chemicals 400.

October 1980

Freeze on new local authority housing in England.

Jobs lost: British Steel 25,000, ICI 4,200, Evening News 1,750, Blue Circle 1,500, Perkins 1,200, Phillips 1,100, Goodyear 1,000, Firestone 600, GKN 644.

November 1980

Limit on public sector pay set at 6 per cent.

Community Land Act repealed, eroding public control of development land.

Contempt of Court Bill published.

Mini budget: spending cuts and tax increases to save £3,000 million.

Jobs lost: Talbot 3,500, ICL 2,500, Bowater 1,600, United Biscuits 1,500.

December 1980

Prescription charges up another 30 p to £1.

Council rents increase of £3.25 announced. Capital spending on council housing cut by 15 per cent.

Jobs lost: Leyland Vehicles 2,700.

January 1981

Green Paper on industrial relations published.

Jobs lost: Vauxhall 5,000, British Shipbuilders 3,200, Tate and Lyle 1,500, Fisons 1,000.

February 1981

Fifty per cent of British Aerospace shares, worth £150 million, sold.

Jobs lost: Talbot 4,800, Courtaulds 1,900, Firth Brown 1,250, Dupont 1,100, London Brick 1,100.

March 1981

Third budget: special tax on windfall bank profits; income tax allowances not increased with inflation.

Privatization of Cable and Wireless announced.

Jobs lost: Lucas Industries 4,500, BPC 2,750.

April 1981

National insurance contributions up 19 per cent to 7.75 per cent.

Jobs lost: Ford plans 29,000 job losses in four years, Lucas Electrical 2,100, Hadfields 1,900.

May 1981

Goverment grant to local authorities to be cut by £900 million.

Jobs lost: Burmah Oil 1,100.

June 1981

Defence White Paper: navy to lose 30,000 jobs, army to lose 7,000. Chatham Dockyard and base to close.

Riots break out on streets of Southhall, Brixton, Manchester, Liverpool and many other cities.

Jobs lost: BR 16,000, ICL 5,200.

July 1981

University places to fall by 12,000 over three years.

Government holdings in British Sugar Corporation sold.

Riots in Toxteth, Liverpool.

British Telecommunications Act.

Employment and Training Act.

National Enterprice Board and National Research and Development Corporation merged to form British Technology Group.

Civil service strike called off after five months.

Jobs lost: Vauxhall 2,000, BP 1,670, British Enkalon 1,300.

August 1981

Jobs lost: Hoover 2,000, Imperial Tobacco 1,000.

September 1981

Jobs lost: British Airways 9,000, ICI 3,000.

October 1981

British Nationality Act — deprives many of citizenship rights.

Sale of Cable and Wireless shares.

Jobs lost: Rolls Royce plans 15,000 cut over five years, Hoover 1,800.

November 1981

Government plans to abolish 16 out of 23 Industrial Training Boards.

New public expenditure plans include rise in council house rents, and cut in real value of unemployment pay.

Jobs lost: Leyland Vehicles 4,100, ICI 1,500.

December 1981

Government launches Youth Training Scheme, to start September 1983.

GLC cheap fares ruled unlawful by Law Lords.

Government plans to cut local authority spending by 3.5 per cent; cut in real terms of £240 million from education budget.

Rise in national insurance surcharge announced.

Jobs lost: British Aluminium 900, Gallagher 800.

January 1982

Unemployment goes over 3 million. Young Workers' Scheme started — employers subsidized for low-paid young workers.

Jobs lost: Rolls Royce 600, Tootal 500.

February 1982

Amersham International sale — speculators make a killing.

Non-EEC overseas visitors to be charged for hospital treatment.

Laker Airways goes bust.

National Freight Corporation sold to consortium of managers.

Jobs lost: Laker Airways 1,700, BSR 1,400, Lucas Aerospace 1,050.

March 1982

Fourth budget maintains squeeze on the economy.

Capital gains tax softened by subtracting gains due to inflation.

Plans to buy Trident II missiles from USA for £7.5 million announced.

Defence review White Paper proposes 10,000 redundancies in Navy over five years.

Jobs lost: Imperial Tobacco 1,700, British Aerospace 1,200.

April 1982

Argentina invades Falklands.

Task force sent.

Prescription charges rise from £1 to £1.30.

Reorganization of British Airways paves way for sell-off.

May 1982

Senior civil servants and army officers get 14.3 per cent pay rise. Judges get 18.69 per cent.

Jobs lost: De Lorean 1,300, British Aerospace 950.

June 1982

Falklands recaptured. Ceasefire on 14 June.

Oil and Gas (Enterprise) Act passed to prepare way for privatization of parts of BNOC and British Gas.

'Assisted area' status removed from several regions.

Proposals to privatize government research and development establishment.

July 1982

Multimillion pound defence purchase programme announced.

Abolition of National Water Council announced.

Eleven new Enterprise Zones created.

HP controls abolished.

Jobs lost: British Airways 7,000, British Shipbuilders 1,500, GEC 800.

August 1982

Jobs lost: British Steel Corporation 1,122.

September 1982

Leak of Think Tank plans to privatize NHS.

October 1982

Pay target of 3.5 per cent set for public sector.

Transport Act.

Jobs lost: RHM 1,300.

November 1982

Mini budget: employers' national insurance surcharge cut 1 per cent; Chancellor proposes to 'claw back' 2 per cent of value of pensions and benefits by failing to cover inflation in 1983.

Jobs lost: British Steel Corporation 3,000, GEC 600, Babcock 480, GKN 440, STC 400, Metal Box 215.

December 1982

Government proposes £31 million development plans for Falklands.

New defence orders for £1 billion to replace equipment lost in Falklands.

Jobs lost: Michelin 4,000, BSC 2,200, BSR 1,100, GEC 600, GKN 550.

January 1983

Serpell Report floats ideas for big cut-backs in British Rail

Announcement of rise in prescription charges from April – up from £1.30 to 1.40.

Green Paper on 'union democracy' published.

Jobs lost: British Shipbuilders 2,300, Ford 1,300, BSC 630, Lucas Girling 550.

February 1983

Public expenditure White Paper: 3 per cent increase in defence spending.

Sale of shares in Associated British Ports.

Jobs lost: BR proposes 3,800, British Alcan 1,200, Distillers 530, Aurora Holdings 200.

March 1983

Budget: small income tax concessions; hidden cut in pensions; nothing to reduce unemployment.

Jobs lost: Littlewoods 1,900, 1,100 dockers from various ports, Woolworth 500.

April 1983

Civil servants offered average of 4.86 per cent – again above the government's 3.5 per cent ceiling.

Over £2 million paid to Falklands Islanders in compensation for Falklands war damage.

National insurance contributions up 9 per cent.

Petrol price rise of 14p a gallon – largest absolute price rise in 90 years. Four star costs about 179p a gallon.

Interest rates/bank base rates cut by half a point to 10 per cent.

Government climbs down over its plans to allow police access to confidential medical and other personal records (Police and Criminal Evidence Bill).

Jobs lost: CEGB 2,000, BS (Cammel Laird) 1,400 at risk, Rank Xerox 1,100, Kraft 940, Alfred Herbert 750, Harland and Wolff 700, Altergo 425, Vosper Thorneycroft 400, Sporting Chronicle 364, Co-op Bank 250, GKN 192, Reed 170, LRC International 160, Racal Avionics 140, BSC 128.

May 1983

Local elections – results from 313 comparable councils in England and Wales. Conservative 518 gains 390 losses; Labour 305 gains 268 losses; Liberal 265 gains 147 losses; SDP 66 gains 74 losses.

Government withdraws £240 million-worth of controversial tax concessions (including the increases in the higher-rate income tax thresholds) to allow the Finance Bill to be rushed through as a result of Labour pressure.

Jobs lost: NCB 1,000, BSC 1,000, BP 1,000 Black and Decker 630, Plessey 400, Timex 300, Cummins 265, Camgears 250, BL 146, Rank 113, Morning Advertiser 83.

June 1983

9 June: Tories win general election. MPs elected: Conservative 397, Labour 209, Alliance 23, SNP 2.

Telecommunications Bill and Police and Criminal

Evidence Bill re-introduced.

Think Tank wound up.

Growth in NHS restricted to 0.5 per cent per annum for next ten years.

UK refund on EEC budget agreed.

Jobs lost: Bird's Eye 2,200, Findus 1,500, Renold 1,200, Weir Engineering Group 430, Schweppes 300.

July 1983

Reduction in local government Rate Support Grant; £280 million cut from grants to mostly Labour-controlled councils.

Cabinet agrees £500 million cuts in public expenditure for the current financial year, including: defence (£240 million), health (£140 million), education (£36 million)

Prevention of Terrorism Bill and London Transport Bill published.

Government sells 7 per cent of shares in BP.

Government reserves right to exclude from NHS pay review any group that takes industrial action.

Thatcher orders 'fundamental re-examination' of welfare spending.

Jobs lost: British Aerospace 3,500, United Glass Containers 818, Goodyear Tyres 700, GEC 700, Rockware Glass 550, BL 400.

August 1983

White Paper on rate-capping published.

British Rail corporate plan published: 1,900 track miles to be cut; 17,000 jobs to go.

Jobs lost: British Rail 17,000, Inland Revenue 4,000, Raleigh 600, John Brown Engineering 500, Metal Box 250.

September 1983

British Technology Group to sell investments.

British Gas forced to dispose of oil assets.

Public sector pay rises in 1984 set at 3 per cent.

Jobs lost: Caterpillar Tractor 960, Rank Xerox 500, STC 390, Metro Cammell 325, GEC 300, Pirelli 170.

October 1983

Bank base rate cut by 0.5 per cent to 9 per cent.

White Paper on abolition of GLC and metropolitan counties published.

Home improvement grants cut from 90 per cent to 75 per cent.

Trade Union Bill published.

Government reduces holding in Cable and Wireless by 50 per cent.

Invasion of Grenada by US.

Resignation of Cecil Parkinson.

Jobs lost: Metal Box 470, SU Butec 300, Adamson and Matchett 250, Rowntree Mackintosh 200.

November 1983

Cruise missiles arrive in UK.

Government forced to withdraw a circular to local authorities seen as foreshadowing a relaxation of the Green Belt policy.

Action against Stock Exchange in Restrictive Practices Court dropped.

Cable and Broadcasting Bill introduced.

Jobs lost: Donald Macpherson 350, BREL 280.

December 1983

Privatization of Ordnance Factories.

White Paper on regional policy published.

Domestic electricity prices increased by 2 per cent.

Domestic gas prices increased by 4–5 per cent.

Bill introduced to stop provision of NHS glasses, and to abolish right of unemployed to claim additional child allowance.

Jobs lost: BSC 360, Diamond Shamrock 200, Perkins 100.

January 1984

Plastic national insurance cards introduced.

GCHQ union ban.

Tory MPs revolt on Rate Bill and housing benefit regulations.

Jobs lost: BREL 3,500, British Shipbuilders 1,870, Leyland Trucks 1,057, Plessey 840, British Aerospace 850, Humber Graving Dock 500, Ferranti 400, BICC 350.

February 1984

Traning for Jobs White Paper published.

Sites of free ports announced.

Government reduces planned cuts in housing benefit.

Changes announced in Crown Agents to prepare way for future privatization

Allegations of left-wing bias in Citizens' Advice Bureaux not substantiated by government inquiry.

Public expenditure White Paper: cuts in school meals, adult education and youth services programmes; expenditure on prisons increased.

Jobs lost: BAT 1,840, Thames Water 1,000, Rank Xerox 550, BSC 430, Rolls Royce 400, Distillers 300.

March 1984

Government announces aid to British Aerospace for A320 Airbus.

Barclays reduce base rate to 8.75 per cent; other banks reduce to 8.5 per cent.

Political curbs on armed forces introduced.

Prescription and dental charges increased; prescriptions by 20 p to £1.60; dental charges by £1 to £14.50.

Jobs lost: Capper Neil 1,000, Lincolnshire County Council 700, Cadbury Schweppes 400, Ley Foundries 300, BSC 215.

April 1984

Government sells publicly owned Scottish airfields.

Manpower Services Commission's plan for the next four years cuts the number of Job Centres to 350.

Share prices drop 20 points on the worst day since 1981.

Government plans to raise £48.5 million through sale of its 48.5 per cent stake in Associated British Ports.

Thatcher declares her intention to seek a third term, claiming that strong government is paying off.

Jobs lost: MSC 1,400, Bradbury Wilkinson 900, Plessey

800, GEC 720, Lucas Electric 700, BICC 570, Lucas 500, Metal Box 304, BSC 176, B.Elliott 150.

May 1984

Local elections: Alliance 204 gains 62 losses; Labour 177 gains 134 losses; Conservatives 130 gains 254 losses. Councillors elected: Labour 1,827; Conservative 1,176; Alliance 432; SNP 62.

New finds boost North Sea Oil reserves.

Banks raise base rates to between 9 and 9.25 per cent.

Police Bill receives its third reading in the Commons.

A House of Commons Select Committee report estimates the cost of Trident at £9.4 billion.

Government legislation to 'unfreeze pensions' is announced.

£4.6 billion wiped off Stock Market in biggest-ever fall in share prices.

Unemployment reaches a record 3.03 million – 12.7 per cent of the labour force.

Jobs lost: BREL 4,200, BL 2,210, British Leyland announces 2,200 jobs to be lost, Hitachi 500, Hongkong and Shanghai Bank 300, Newton Chambers 198, Daview, Pritchard and Richmond 167, Thomas Rochford 120, Ransome and Rapier 100.

June 1984

14 June: EEC election result: Conservatives 45, Labour 32, Alliance 1, SNP 1.

Five per cent rise in postal charges announced for September.

Demonstration against President Reagan's visit to Britain draws 200,000.

The Rates Act receives the Royal Assent.

The London Regional Transport Act removes control of London Transport from the GLC.

Government sells Enterprise Oil by tender on the Stock Market – the first sale in the privatization programme for 1984.

Jobs lost: Matchbox 1,250, Bartons 600, Army workshops 600, BSC 550, British Bakeries 400, BS 383, Lear Fan

300, Sumitomo 300, Whitbread 300, Telffer 287, Priestman 250, John Moores 100, NAM Special Vehicles 80, Wirral Newspapers 67, ICI 60.

July 1984

Sterling falls to a record low against the US dollar at $1.334.

The base rate rises to 12 per cent, making the real cost of borrowing the highest this century.

High Court sets aside the government ban on unions at GCHQ – the government gets the right to appeal.

Government announces its decision to sell British Rail's Sealink division.

The Environment Secretary declares his list of 18 local authorities due to be rate-capped under new legislation.

The government announces plans to sell seven British Shipbuilders yards.

The Trade Union Act receives the Royal Assent.

Jobs lost: Herefordshire, Herefordshire and Worcester councils 1,000, Milk Marketing Board 412, BT 392, Molins 350, Jeyes 300, Associated Passenger Transport 150, Portakabin 50.

August 1984

Medical Research Council is forced to close three medical research units due to lack of government funds.

The Department of Environment plans a £1 million campaign to advertise the merits of council house sales.

Government floats British Leyland's Jaguar Division on the Stock Market.

Jobs lost: Distillers 715, NEI 525, Royal Navy 515, Metal Box 346, Metro-Camell 270, Robert Jenkins 240, Mersyside-food 158, Rubery Owen 150, BSC 70.

September 1984

The pound falls to $1.23.

A Department of Environment document discloses that Labour councils have 'unintentionally' been deprived of £50 million.

Johnson Matthey Bank collapses and is purchased by the Bank of England.

Unemployment reaches 13.6 per cent of the labour force.

The balance-of-payments deficit on current account reaches a record £514 million.

Jobs lost: NEI 1,500, Automotive Products 1,000, Shell 590, STC 450, Reed 400, Stag 340, Foster Wheeler 90, GEC-Marconi 55, Slingsby 50, Mercantile Credit (Barclays) 50.

October 1984

Government launches a £500,000 campaign to support its rate-capping policy.

White Paper preparing for privatization of British Airways is published.

Leon Brittan announces new resources for the battle against the miners' strike.

Sterling falls to $1.19.

British Rail announces its corporate plan which threatens 13,000 redundancies over five years.

Some Tories revolt against the government's plan to impose cuts in housing benefit.

Sixteen Labour councils due for the government rate-capping control decide to defy the law.

Jobs lost: Swan Hunter 2,000, Littlewoods 600, Molins 440, BSC 400, Metal Box 350, Southampton Docks 165, Shell 110, Mirrlees 93, Aston Martin 58.

November 1984

Defence Secretay refuses demands for a White Paper on the events surrounding the sinking of the Argentine cruiser *General Belgrano*.

Chancellor's autumn statement promises tax cuts totalling £1.5 billion for spring 1985.

Train fares to rise by 8 per cent in the new year.

Government sells off British Telecom.

House of Lords upholds the government's decision to ban unions at GCHQ.

Government cuts £340 million in regional development aid.

Police and Criminal Evidence Bill receives the Royal Assent.

Jobs lost: British Shipbuilders 2,890, Royal Ordnance Factories 1,819, Hoover 500, BSC 300, Courtaulds 100, RA Lister 97, Morning Advertiser 65, Rowntree Mackintosh 50.

December 1984

Tory backbenchers revolt against the Education Secretary's proposal that parents should pay a substantial new share of university student fees and maintenance. Joseph eventually backs down, but cuts science budget by £11 million to meet the cost.

Social Services Secretary announces a clamp-down on supplementary benefit spending on board and lodging.

British Telecom shares show 90 per cent premium on debut on the Stock Exchange.

New housing investment rules will halve the amount of reserve money councils can spend on council house-building.

Tory backbenchers revolt over Patrick Jenkin's announcement of council housing cuts.

Jobs lost: Michelin 2,600, Vauxhall 700, Borg-Warner 690, BICC 430, Cape Insulation 400, Coles Cranes 400, Trafalgar House 300, Cold Shield 230, STC 230, Kodak 160, Tomatin 60.

Index

Index

OTHER BOOKS FROM PLUTO

WORLD VIEW 1985

Edited by Pete Ayrton, Tom Engelhardt and Vron Ware

The radical yearbook: *World View 1985* is a collaboration between publishers in the United States, Britain, France, Italy and Germany. Divided into sections — world politics; the state; ecology and the environment; war and peace; capital and labour; culture and ideology; hot spots plus; and extensive world table — articles include: 'Cold War II'; 'A Mixed Year for the Peace Movements'; 'Migrant Workers in Western Europe'; 'Is Thatcherism Rational?'; 'Style as Industry'; 'The Revival of Christianity'; 'The Growing Concentration in Industry'; 'Gay Culture'; 'Central America Under Fire'; 'The Films of George Lucas'.

Amongst the contributors are Teresa Hayter, Fred Halliday, Barbara Ehrenreich, Stephen Castles, Richard Hart, Anthony Barnet, Mike Kidron, Ronald Segal, Pete Biskind and Bobbie Jacobson.

224 pages
0 86104 665 X   **£5.95 paperback**

ORGANISING THINGS:
A GUIDE TO SUCCESSFUL
POLITICAL ACTION
SUE WARD

Organising Things is the first comprehensive
guide to practical political action. Packed
with information and handy checklists, this
book takes the tears out of organizing: public
meetings — how to chair them, how to
steward them; marches and demonstrations
— how to plan them, how to deal with the
police; lobbies — how to arrange mass
events; petitions — how to get people to sign;
conferences — what to provide and where to
book; festivals, fetes and bazaars — how to
finance them and what to lay on.

The book shows how to get funds, publicity,
help, and information. Sue Ward explains how
to design, produce, and distribute leaflets and
posters, and develop your own ideas for
publicity. This books tells you all about the
law you need to know, and how to cope with
disasters.

In fact, it has everything you need to make a
success of *Organising Things*.

288 pages. Index
0 86104 799 0   £4.95

THE COHABITATION
HANDBOOK
A WOMEN'S GUIDE TO THE LAW
ANNE BOTTOMLEY, KATHERINE GIEVE,
GAY MOON and ANGELA WEIR

Second edition revised and updated

This new edition, completely revised and
updated, is a practical guide to the law for
women who are living with someone without
being married. It covers such issues as whose
name to take; whose place the rented or
bought home is; homelessness; domestic
violence; the cost of living together; the
problems of bringing up the children; and, in
addition, offers some very useful legal advice,
and further reading.

256 pages. Index
0 86104 793 1   £5.50 paperback

GET IT ON . . . RADIO AND TELEVISION
JANE DRINKWATER

Get It On is a practical guide to getting airtime — 'access' programmes, spots for appeals and announcements, news slots, documentaries and phone-ins are described.

The book is a directory of London's local broadcast media. It also includes networked outlets in BBC, Channel 4 and ITV. There are around 100 detailed programme reports, and it tells you how to use who, what, where, and when.

Containing unique information on programmes and contacts, and providing names and addresses of companies, their executive personnel, the names of editors of the major programmes, programme-transmission times, editorial schedules, special interests, programme developments, structure and content, *Get It On* is an essential tool for all community, voluntary, political, Trade Union, and special-interest groups who should be using the media. Dealing mainly with London, the information has application throughout the country.

272 pages. Index
0 86104 785 0   £3.95 paperback

WOMEN AND HARASSMENT AT WORK
NATHALIE HADJIFOTIOU

This is the first detailed guide to ways of tackling sexual harassment at work. It is packed full of practical advice, ideas and examples for campaigning and negotiating in both union and non-union workplaces. It explains where to get help and how to use the law.

208 pages. Index
0 86104 729 X   £3.95 paperback

RIGHTS AT WORK

JEREMY McMULLEN

Second Edition

Completely revised and greatly expanded, this well-known, authoritative guide to employment law explains and shows how to use workers' rights — it covers everything from unfair dismissal to secondary action, redundancy to equal rights. All the major changes introduced by the last government are here, together with suggestions about how to fight them.

The book supersedes the author's earlier *Employment Law Under the Tories*.

'Easily the most accurate, comprehensive and best-written explanation of employment law rights designed for union activists; every shop steward will want a copy.' *Industrial Relations Review and Report*

560 pages. Index
0 86104 730 3   £7.95 paperback

Pluto books are available through your local bookshop. In case of difficulty contact Pluto to find out local stockists or to obtain catalogues/leaflets (telephone 01-482 1973).
   If all else fails write to:

Pluto Press Limited
Freepost (no stamp required)
105A Torriano Avenue
London NW5 1YP

To order, enclose a cheque/p.o. payable to Pluto Press to cover price of book, plus 50p per book for postage and packing (£2.50 maximum).